EMPOWER

SECOND EDITION

WORKBOOK

WITHOUT ANSWERS

A2

ELEMENTARY

Peter Anderson

CONTENTS

2

Contents

1A | I'M FROM FRANCE

1 GRAMMAR be: positive and negative

a Underline the correct forms of the verb be.

1 I 's / 're / 'm Brazilian.
2 They 're / 'm / 's from Barcelona.
3 He 're / 's / 'm with his Spanish friends.
4 We 's / 'm / 're American.
5 Rome 'm / 're / 's a beautiful city.
6 It 're / 's / 'm very hot in August.

b Complete each sentence with a negative form of the verb be. Use contractions. (Sometimes there is more than one possible answer.)

1 The Italian team _isn't / 's not_ very good at the moment.
2 My brother _____ at the party. He's here.
3 My sister and I _____ Brazilian. We're Mexican.
4 I _____ Spanish. I'm Italian.
5 They _____ from Rome. They're from Milan.
6 Tomomi _____ Chinese. She's Japanese.
7 You _____ from Hamburg. You're from Berlin.
8 Mike _____ at a party. He's at a concert.

2 VOCABULARY
Countries and nationalities

a Complete the sentences with the correct nationalities.

I'm from Italy.

1 He's   _Italian_   .

I'm from Brazil.

2 She's _____ .

I'm from Turkey.

3 He's _____ .

We're from Mexico.

4 They're _____ .

I'm from Russia.

I'm from Spain.

5 She's _____ .

6 She's _____ .

I'm from China.

We're from Saudi Arabia.

7 She's _____ .

8 They're _____ .

---

b Complete the crossword puzzle.

→ Across

4 Argentina, Brazil and Venezuela are all in
____South____ ____America____ .
7 _____ is the home of flamenco dancing and paella.
10 Mount Fuji is in _____ .
11 Paris, Lyon and Marseilles are all in _____ .

↓ Down

1 Rio de Janeiro is in _____ .
2 Moscow is the capital city of _____ .
3 Wolfgang, Hans and Petra are from Berlin in _____ .
5 Sydney and Melbourne are cities in _____ .
6 Florence, Rome and Venice are all in _____ .
8 The capital of _____ is Bangkok.
9 The capital of _____ isn't Istanbul. It's Ankara.

```
                                    [1]
        [2]           [3]
[4]S O U T H [5]A M E R [6]I C A
[7]
      [8]
                         [9]
[10]
         [11]
```

3 PRONUNCIATION Syllables and word stress

a ▶01.01 Listen and complete the chart with the words in the box. Then underline the stressed syllable in each word.

~~Turkish~~ Iranian Irish Japanese Saudi American Russian Mexican Nigerian Colombian

2 syllables	3 syllables	4 syllables
Turkish		

4

1B | SHE'S A LOVELY PERSON

1 GRAMMAR
be: questions and short answers

a <u>Underline</u> the correct words to complete the questions.

1 Where *you are* / <u>*are you*</u> / *is you* from?
2 *Is he* / *He is* / *Are he* married?
3 *Are she* / *She is* / *Is she* from Mexico?
4 *You are* / *You is* / *Are you* here with your family?
5 *Is you* / *Are you* / *You are* Turkish?
6 What *their names are* / *is their names* / *are their names*?
7 *Are Enzo* / *Is Enzo* / *Enzo is* Spanish?
8 *Is Joe and Mel* / *Joe and Mel are* / *Are Joe and Mel* American?

b Complete each short answer with the correct form of *be*. Use contractions where possible. (Sometimes there is more than one possible answer.)

1 **A** Are you Brazilian?
  B Yes, ____I am____.
2 **A** Is David a good tennis player?
  B No, _____.
3 **A** Are you and your brother here on holiday?
  B No, _____.
4 **A** Is Antalya a friendly city?
  B Yes, _____.
5 **A** Are you from Mexico City?
  B No, _____.
6 **A** Is Julia Australian?
  B Yes, _____.
7 **A** Are your friends cool?
  B Yes, _____.
8 **A** Are Alan and Sue here today?
  B No, _____.

2 VOCABULARY Adjectives

a ▶ 01.02 Listen and complete the sentences with the words in the box.

great fantastic cool brilliant lovely ~~warm~~ friendly pleasant kind well-known quiet popular

1 I like Beatriz. She's a __warm__ and _____ person.
2 Our new teacher's really _____ and he's very _____ with his students.
3 Taylor Swift's a very _____ singer. Her new song's _____!
4 My friend Dani's a _____ person. She's really _____ to all her friends.
5 Dusit is very _____, but he's a _____ friend.
6 Mr Jones is a very _____ person and he's a _____ teacher.

b Complete the sentences with the words in 2a.

1 New York is a f<u>antast</u>ic city. I love it!
2 My father's a b_____t doctor.
3 He's a very w_____l-k_____n singer in my country. He's really p_____r with young people.
4 I think your brother's really c_____l. He's a g_____t guitarist.
5 My friend Ana's very f_____y. She's a really l_____y person.
6 John's a very q_____t person. He's always k_____d to animals.

3 PRONUNCIATION
Sound and spelling: /k/

a Do the words in the chart have a /k/ sound? Put a tick (✓) in the correct column.

	/k/ sound	No /k/ sound
chat		✓
cake		
keep		
know		
quiz		
capital		
bike		
chart		

b ▶ 01.03 Listen and check.

1C EVERYDAY ENGLISH
What's your surname?

1 USEFUL LANGUAGE
Asking for and giving information

a Put the words in the correct order to make sentences.

1 help / I / can / how / ?
<u>How can I help?</u>

2 to do / like / I'd / a fitness class .
_____

3 surname / your / what's ?
_____

4 you / please / spell / sorry – / that, / can ?
_____

5 class / the / time's / next / what ?
_____

6 at / tomorrow / it's / half past six .
_____

7 class / the / where's ?
_____

8 Studio / 3 / in / it's .
_____

9 6:30 / in / that's / Studio / 3 / so ?
_____

10 help / for / thanks / your .
_____

11 welcome / you're .
_____

b ▶ 01.04 Listen and check.

c Put the conversation in the correct order.

- [ ] No problem.
- [ ] Cumberbatch.
- [ ] When are the classes?
- [1] Hello. How can I help?
- [ ] They're on Mondays at 7:30.
- [ ] Certainly. What's your surname?
- [ ] Sorry – can you spell that, please?
- [ ] Hi. I'd like to do a German class. I'm a beginner.
- [ ] Great. Can I book a place on the course?
- [ ] Thank you. Enjoy the class.
- [ ] C-U-M-B-E-R-B-A-T-C-H.

d ▶ 01.05 Listen and check.

2 PRONUNCIATION
Intonation for checking; Consonant clusters

a ▶ 01.06 Listen to each speaker. Does the intonation go up (↗) or down (↘)? Tick (✓) the correct box.

		↗	↘
1	Certainly.	☐	✓
2	Good idea.	☐	☐
3	Sorry?	☐	☐
4	Me?	☐	☐
5	Sure.	☐	☐
6	Off to the gym?	☐	☐
7	Of course.	☐	☐
8	Is he from London?	☐	☐
9	Yes, he is.	☐	☐
10	Is she Italian?	☐	☐
11	No, she isn't.	☐	☐
12	No problem.	☐	☐

b ▶ 01.07 Listen and write the number of consonant sounds in each word.

1	[2] three	6	☐ match
2	☐ eight	7	☐ brother
3	☐ twelve	8	☐ warm
4	☐ sixteen	9	☐ kitchen
5	☐ right	10	☐ well-known

1D SKILLS FOR WRITING
I'm Carla and I'm from Italy

1 READING

a Andrea is on an English course in Melbourne. Read his fact file on the language school website and tick (✓) the correct answers.

1 Which country is Andrea from?
- a ☐ Spain
- b ☐ Australia
- c ☐ France
- d ☐ Italy

2 Which city is Andrea from?
- a ☐ Melbourne
- b ☐ Rome
- c ☐ Milan
- d ☐ Madrid

b Read Andrea's personal profile. Are the sentences true (*T*) or false (*F*)?

1 Andrea's 20 years old.
2 Andrea studies in Milan.
3 Andrea's in Australia with friends from Bologna.
4 Andrea's on a computer course in Melbourne.
5 Andrea likes listening to music.

FACT FILE

 Name: Andrea Rossi

 Age: 20

 Nationality: Italian

 Lives in: Bologna

 Hometown: Milan

 Job/Occupation: Student, University of Bologna

Likes: languages, music, running

Personal profile

This is Andrea Rossi. He's 20 years old and he's Italian. He's from Milan, but he studies at the University of Bologna. It's his first time in Australia, and he's on an English course in Melbourne with a big group of friends from Bologna. He's very happy to be in Melbourne. He likes languages, music and running.

2 WRITING SKILLS
Capital letters and punctuation

a Correct the personal profile about Carlos. Add capital letters and punctuation (.,').

Personal profile

This is carlos ferreira hes 35 years old and hes brazilian hes from petrópolis but he studies languages hes on a spanish course in bogotá this isnt his first time in colombia hes very happy to be in bogotá he likes languages the cinema and jazz

This is _____
_____
_____
_____
_____
_____
_____
_____
_____
_____
_____

3 WRITING

a Complete the fact file with information about a friend, a family member or a famous person.

FACT FILE

 Name: _____

 Age: _____

Nationality: _____

Lives in: _____

Hometown: _____

Job/Occupation: _____

Likes: _____

b Use the information in the fact file to write a personal profile about this person. Remember to use capital letters and punctuation in the correct places.

This is _____
_____
_____
_____
He/She likes _____
_____
_____
_____

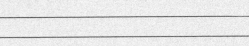

1 READING

a Read the letter. What are these parts of the letter about? Tick (✓) the correct answers.

Paragraph 1 is about …
a ☐ Elena's dogs.
b ✓ Elena and her mum.
c ☐ Elena's sister.
d ☐ Elena's dad.

Paragraph 2 is about …
a ☐ Elena's dogs.
b ☐ Elena and her mum.
c ☐ Elena's sister.
d ☐ Elena's dad.

Paragraph 3 is about …
a ☐ Elena's dogs.
b ☐ Elena and her mum.
c ☐ Elena's sister.
d ☐ Elena's dad.

Paragraph 4 is about …
a ☐ Elena's dogs.
b ☐ Elena and her mum.
c ☐ Elena's sister.
d ☐ Elena's dad.

b Read the letter again. Are the sentences true (*T*) or false (*F*)?

1 The letter is to Elena's Mexican friend.
2 Elena's mum's family lives in Mexico.
3 Elena's dad is horrible.
4 Elena and her family go to Mexico every year.
5 Elena's mum's family has a lot of money.
6 Elena's sister isn't very good at tennis.
7 Elena loves her dogs.
8 Elena wants Laila to write to her again.

c Write a letter to a new friend in China.
- Write about each person in your family.
- How many people live in your house? Who are they?
- Where does your family go on holiday?

Dear _____
_____
_____
_____
_____
_____
_____
_____
_____
_____
_____
_____

Dear Laila,

Thanks for your letter. It's really interesting for me to hear about your life in Turkey.

1 Here is a photo of my family. It's quite a new photo, so you can see what we all look like. As you can see, I have dark hair, and so does my mum. She's from Mexico.

2 My dad's quite quiet, but he's very kind, and he often helps me with my homework. He's Irish – that's why we live here in Cork. Every summer we visit my mum's family in Mexico. Her parents aren't rich, but they have a lovely house near the beach. I love it!

3 You can see my sister next to me. She has a lot of friends – she's very popular. She's also a brilliant tennis player. In fact, she isn't at home very often because she plays tennis so much!

4 At the front of the photo, you can see two other important members of our family. They're very old and they aren't very clean, but I love them. They're my dogs, Benny and Jerry!

Write back soon and tell me more about your family!

Best wishes,

Elena

2 LISTENING

a ▶ 01.08 Listen to the conversation. Tick (✓) the best endings for the sentences.

1 Kerem and Pedro …
   a ☐ know each other well.
   b ✓ don't know each other well.

2 They go to …
   a ☐ the same football club.
   b ☐ the same school.

3 Kerem says that Pedro …
   a ☐ can go to the next football match with him.
   b ☐ can take him to the next football match.

b ▶ 01.08 Listen to the conversation again. Complete the sentences with the words in the box.

doesn't have   plays   ready   speaks
match   ~~football~~   grandma   Spanish

1 Pedro and Kerem meet at a ___football___ club.
2 Pedro is from Segovia. He's _____.
3 Kerem's _____ is also Spanish.
4 Kerem _____ Spanish, but not very well.
5 Kerem _____ football with the club every week.
6 The _____ next week is in Bolu.
7 Pedro _____ a car.
8 Pedro must be _____ by 9 o'clock.

c Write a conversation between two people who meet each other. Remember to say:

- where they are from
- what they like doing in their free time.

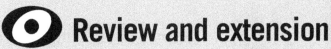

Review and extension

1 GRAMMAR

<u>Underline</u> and correct the mistake in each sentence.

1 My mother and father <u>is</u> from Kolkata. *are*
2 She really's friendly.
3 Daniela are Italian.
4 Im' from Bangkok, the capital of Thailand.
5 You are American or Canadian?
6 There from San Francisco.
7 **A** Is you and your friends Turkish?
   B No, we not.
8 **A** Are Maria from Rio de Janeiro?
   B Yes, she's.

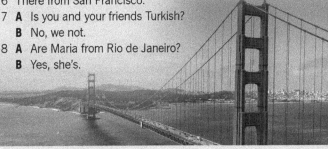

2 VOCABULARY

Correct the mistake in each sentence.

1 My holiday in Jamaica was wonderfull. *wonderful*
2 New York is an amaizing city!
3 My best friend Nick's a really kool guy.
4 The weather is terible, but our holiday is great!
5 This is Anna. She's very frendly.
6 My mum likes Michael. She thinks he's very neice!
7 Dubai's a fantastik place to visit.
8 His uncle is pour, but he's very happy.

3 WORDPOWER *from*

Match 1–6 with a–f to make sentences.

1 My sister and I are
2 Dinner is
3 The station is about 2 km
4 Are you
5 The next yoga class is
6 The train

a from Glasgow is now at Platform 25.
b from 10:30 to 12:00 in the gym.
c from Washington or New York?
d from our hotel.
e from Australia.
f from 7:00 to 10:00 at the Sorrento Restaurant.

◑ REVIEW YOUR PROGRESS

Look again at Review your progress on p. 18 of the Student's Book. How well can you do these things now?
3 = very well   2 = well   1 = not so well

I CAN …	
talk about where I'm from	☐
talk about people I know	☐
ask for and give information	☐
write an online profile.	☐

2A | SHE LOVES HER JOB

1 GRAMMAR Present simple: positive and negative

a Underline the correct words to complete the sentences.

1 I'm a nurse in a hospital, so I often *works* / <u>*work*</u> / *working* at night.
2 We're always really busy, so we *don't have* / *doesn't have* / *not have* time to go to the supermarket during the week.
3 Jake studies hard in the morning, so he *relax* / *relaxing* / *relaxes* for half an hour after lunch.
4 Sonia *not have* / *don't have* / *doesn't have* a very interesting job.
5 Joe's not very interested in sport, so he *doesn't watch* / *don't watch* / *watch not* football matches on TV.
6 We work hard during the week, so we usually *relaxes* / *relax* / *relaxing* at the weekend.

b Complete the sentences with the correct forms of the verbs in brackets. Use contractions where possible.

1 My father <u>*doesn't drive*</u> (not drive) to work. He always <u>*goes*</u> (go) by bus.
2 She _____ (not like) her job because she _____ (not make) much money.
3 I _____ (not like) my university maths course because I _____ (think) it's really boring.
4 My journey to work only _____ (take) about 20 minutes, and I usually _____ (start) work at 8:30.

2 VOCABULARY Jobs

a Complete the crossword puzzle.

→ Across
1 Carol works as a <u>*tour guide*</u> at Edinburgh Castle.
4 My sister's a _____ _____, so some people think her job is very dangerous.
6 A typical London _____ _____ drives for eight hours a day.
7 A _____ works in a hospital.
8 My dad is a _____ for Singapore Airlines.
9 David's a well-known _____. He lives in Hollywood now.

↓ Down
2 The _____ at this hotel is really friendly and helpful.
3 He's a famous _____ and he works in a really expensive restaurant in Paris.
4 Magazines use a _____ to take photos of famous people.
5 My brother works at the Volkswagen garage as a _____.

3 PRONUNCIATION Word stress

a ▶02.01 Which syllable is stressed in the words in **bold**? Listen and tick (✓) the correct stress.

1 She works as a **receptionist** in a big hotel.
  a ✓ recep<u>tionist</u>   b ☐ recept<u>ionist</u>
2 He's a Russian **businessman**.
  a ☐ <u>business</u>man   b ☐ business<u>man</u>
3 My father's an **engineer**.
  a ☐ eng<u>ineer</u>   b ☐ engin<u>eer</u>
4 Jack works as a **mechanic** for Mercedes.
  a ☐ <u>mechanic</u>   b ☐ mec<u>hanic</u>
5 My uncle's a **taxi driver** in London.
  a ☐ taxi <u>driver</u>   b ☐ <u>taxi</u> driver
6 Brad Pitt's a well-known American **actor**.
  a ☐ <u>actor</u>   b ☐ ac<u>tor</u>
7 My **secretary** speaks excellent English.
  a ☐ <u>secret</u>ary   b ☐ secre<u>tary</u>
8 She works as a **tour guide** in Rome.
  a ☐ tour <u>guide</u>   b ☐ <u>tour</u> guide
9 He's a very friendly **police officer**.
  a ☐ <u>police</u> officer   b ☐ police <u>officer</u>
10 Where's the **photographer**?
  a ☐ <u>photo</u>grapher   b ☐ pho<u>tographer</u>

4 PRONUNCIATION -s endings

a ▶02.02 Listen and complete the chart with the verbs in the box.

~~watches~~ likes goes stops uses finishes
plays teaches works freezes

The verb has an extra syllable: /ɪz/	The verb doesn't have an extra syllable: /s/ or /z/
watches	

2B | DO YOU WORRY ABOUT EXAMS?

1 GRAMMAR Present simple: questions and short answers

a Underline the correct words to complete the sentences.

1 **A** *You like / Do you like / Like you* your new job?
   B Yes, *I does / I like / I do.*
2 **A** *Study Azra / Azra studies / Does Azra study* on Sundays?
   B No, *she no studies / she doesn't / she don't.*
3 What *do they do / do they / they do* in their free time?
4 How many hours a week *study you / you study / do you study* English?
5 **A** *Does he have / He has / Has he* important exams at school this year?
   B Yes, *he has / he does / he is.*
6 **A** *Listen you / Do you listen / You listen* to podcasts while you study?
   B No, *I not listen / I listen not / I don't.*

b Put the words in the correct order to make questions.

1 you / in your free time / do / what / do ?
   <u>What do you do in your free time?</u>
2 you / study / do / for your exams / late at night ?
   _____
3 you / music / do / while you study / to / listen ?
   _____
4 at the end / exams / have / do / of this year / they / important ?
   _____
5 to / go / how many days a week / she / does / university ?
   _____

2 VOCABULARY Studying

a Complete the sentences with the words in the box.

timetable   break   notes   mark   studies   exams   ~~term~~

1 At our school the summer ____term____ is 12 weeks long.
2 I hate _____ because I'm not very good at them.
3 Jun-ho has a new _____ for his English course. He has classes on Mondays, Wednesdays and Fridays from 11:30 to 1:00.
4 Sofia always gets a good _____ in her maths tests. She's brilliant at maths!
5 It's important to take _____ in your notebook when you are in your English lessons.
6 The computer class is from 9:30 to 12:30, but we usually have a _____ at 11 o'clock.
7 Your computer _____ are very important.

3 VOCABULARY Time

a Match the clocks with the times in the box.

a quarter to nine   half past nine   five to nine
twenty-five past nine   a quarter past nine
~~five past nine~~   nine o'clock   twenty-five to nine

1 <u>five past nine</u>   2 _____

3 _____   4 _____

5 _____   6 _____

7 _____   8 _____

2C | EVERYDAY ENGLISH
I'd like a latte

1 USEFUL LANGUAGE
Asking for things and replying

a Match sentences 1–5 with responses a–e.

1 [c] Could I come to your place tonight?
2 [ ] Can I phone you tomorrow?
3 [ ] I'd like some help with my car.
4 [ ] Can I have a hot chocolate, please?
5 [ ] Could we meet at 4:15?

a Of course. Small or large?
b Sure. Is it in the car park?
c Sorry, we're not at home.
d Sorry, I've got a meeting at 4 o'clock.
e Sure, no problem. Call me around 10 o'clock.

2 PRONUNCIATION
Sound and spelling: *ou*

a ▶02.04 Listen to the words with *ou* and complete the table with the words in the box.

pound journey tour fought our flavour

Sound 1 /ə/ (e.g. *colour*)	Sound 2 /ɔː/ (e.g. *course*)	Sound 3 /aʊ/ (e.g. *house*)
		pound

b Complete the short conversations with the words in the box.

sorry   could you   I'd like   I'm really   ~~can I have~~
doesn't matter   of course   a pity   no problem
could we

1 **A** _____Can I have_____ a coffee, please?
  B _____. White or black?
2 **A** _____ some help with my homework, please.
  B _____, not now. I'm busy.
  A That's OK. It _____.
3 **A** _____ pass me my phone, please?
  B Sure, _____. Here you are.
4 **A** _____ meet tomorrow morning?
  B _____ sorry. I'm not free.
  A Oh, well, that's _____.

c ▶02.03 Listen and check.

2D | SKILLS FOR WRITING
I need English for my job

1 READING

a Read Juliana's competition entry form and tick (✓) the reason she needs English in her job.

1. ☐ Because she now works in Rio Grande.
2. ☐ Because she has a new job in the hotel.
3. ☐ Because the hotel guests don't all speak Portuguese.
4. ☐ Because her manager doesn't speak English.

b Read the competition entry form again. Are the sentences true (*T*) or false (*F*)?

1. Juliana doesn't like working as a hotel receptionist.
2. The guests want to speak Portuguese to her.
3. Sometimes it's hard for her to understand the guests.
4. She doesn't need to use the phone very much.
5. She would like to learn more words so she can help tourists.

2 WRITING SKILLS Spelling

a Correct the spelling of the words in **bold**.

1. What's your home **adress**, please? ___address___
2. Luisa **nose** a lot about computers. _____
3. We always have a **brake** for 15 minutes in the middle of our English lesson. _____
4. I think it's very **dificult** to study Spanish and Portuguese at the same time. _____
5. What time do you want to **meat** me after work? _____
6. I would like to see the new James Bond film next **weak**. _____
7. My **farther** works as a doctor in Auckland. _____

3 WRITING

a Luis Silva is a business student from Portugal. He studies English and Business in Swansea. There is a competition to win ten free language lessons. Use the information below to complete the entry form for him.

Personal information

Email: silva_l@cup.org
Class: 8B
Course start date: 09/01/24
Hometown: Braga, Portugal
Job: Business student
Why he needs English: make friends, read books, pass a business exam in English
Problems: some difficult words, people speak fast
Wants to improve: listening, speaking, writing essays (spelling is difficult!)

Competition entry form

First name:	Juliana		Last name:	Gomes

Gender: ✓ female ☐ male   Nationality: Brazilian

Your class now: 8C   Class start date: 05/04/24

Why is English important for you?

I work as a hotel receptionist in Rio de Janeiro. I like my job. I'm always busy and the guests are nice and friendly. But most of them don't speak very good Portuguese. They all want to speak in English and my English isn't very good.

What's difficult for you?

The guests speak quickly and I don't understand them. It's difficult to answer. So learning English is very important for my job.

What do you want to improve in your English?

I use the phone a lot at work, so I need to improve my listening and speaking. I also want to improve my grammar and learn more vocabulary to help tourists in my city. I'd like to stay in the USA for another month to improve my English.

SWANSEA UNIVERSITY LANGUAGE CENTRE COMPETITION ENTRY FORM

First name: ....   Last name: ....
Gender: ○ female ○ male   Nationality: ....
Email: ....   Class: ....

Why is English important for you?

English is important for me because ....
....
....

What's difficult for you?

....
....
....

What do you want to improve in your English?

....
....
....

1 READING

a Read the text and <u>underline</u> the correct words to complete the sentences.

1 Irene <u>likes</u> / *doesn't like* her job.
2 She *wants* / *doesn't want* to be a cleaner for her whole life.
3 She *works* / *doesn't work* the whole day.

b Complete the sentences about the text. Use the words in the box.

> at the end of the day   ~~early in the morning~~
> in the afternoon   in the middle of the day

1 Irene starts work *early in the morning*.
2 She finishes work _____.
3 She goes to college _____.
4 She does her college work _____.

c Read the text again. Are the sentences true (*T*) or false (*F*)?

1 Irene thinks that most people want to be a cleaner.
2 There are a lot of people and cars in the streets at 6 o'clock in the morning.
3 Irene likes to hear the birds.
4 She doesn't do very much at work.
5 She talks to the nurses in the hospital.
6 She wants to be a doctor.
7 She studies at a college.
8 She doesn't have time for her studies.

d Write a paragraph about one job you want to do and one job you don't want to do. Think about these questions:

• What are the good things about the job you want to do? Why do you like those things?
• What are the bad things about the job you don't want to do? Why don't you like those things?

Irene's story

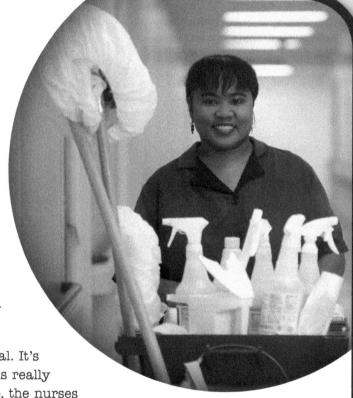

I'm a cleaner. I love my job. I'm sure you're surprised to hear that. You probably don't know anyone who wants to become a cleaner!

So why do I love my job? Well, first, I start work at 6 o'clock. When I walk to work, the streets are quiet and I can hear the birds sing. You don't usually hear the birds in the middle of the city!

The second thing is, I work in a hospital. It's hard work, but I know that what I do is really useful, and that makes me happy. Also, the nurses are friendly, and I chat with them when I have time.

But I don't want to be a cleaner all my life. I really want to be an engineer. I go to college in the evenings to study.

That's why the third reason is the really important one. I finish work at lunch time! So when everyone else goes back to work after their lunch break, I have time for my studies.

2 LISTENING

a ▶ **02.05** Listen to the conversation. Tick (✓) the things Alex and Dan talk about.

- ✓ school
- ☐ exams
- ☐ sport
- ☐ food
- ☐ jobs
- ☐ their dads

b Complete the sentences about the conversation. Use *wants* or *doesn't want*.

1 Alex _doesn't want_ to work in his dad's shop.
2 Alex _____ more time to study.
3 Dan _____ to study less.
4 Dan _____ to be a pilot.
5 Dan _____ to be a photographer.
6 Dan _____ to take photos of famous people.
7 Dan's dad _____ to pay for him to become a photographer.
8 Dan _____ Alex to say the same things as his dad.

c Write a conversation between two people talking about their studies and what jobs they want to do. Think about these questions:

- Do they work hard?
- Do they enjoy their studies?
- What job do they want to do?
- Do their parents agree?

◉ Review and extension

1 GRAMMAR

Correct the sentences.

1 They starts work at 9:00 on Saturdays.
   They start work at 9:00 on Saturdays.
2 Mei study hard at the weekend.
3 She speak Portuguese and Spanish very well.
4 Stefano and Erik doesn't likes exams.
5 Do she finish work late?
6 Does Jacob and Sara have a maths class at 2:30?
7 My father work as a taxi driver.
8 We knows a lot about computers.

2 VOCABULARY

Correct the sentences.

1 My maneger is great. She's a very kind person.
   My manager is great. She's a very kind person.
2 Mrs Carr works as a recepsionist at the hospital.
3 He's a Korean businesman.
4 My cousin's a police in the USA.
5 Graciela Iturbide's a famous Mexican fotograf.
6 Max works at a five-star hotel as a sheff.
7 The drivers taxi in Istanbul always go very fast.
8 My friend's a mekanik and he fixes my old car for free.

3 WORDPOWER *work*

Underline the correct words to complete the sentences.

1 I *start / go* work at 8:30 in the morning.
2 My father works *for / as* a sales manager *for / in* Speedy Computer Solutions.
3 Silvia works *for / as* a nurse *as / in* a big hospital in Hong Kong.
4 I need to find a new job because I'm *at / out of* work at the moment.
5 Sorry, I can't text you when I'm *at / in* work.
6 Sometimes I *go to / go* work by car, but I usually walk.

◔ REVIEW YOUR PROGRESS

Look again at Review your progress on p. 28 of the Student's Book. How well can you do these things now?
3 = very well   2 = well   1 = not so well

I CAN ...	
talk about jobs	☐
talk about study habits	☐
ask for things and reply	☐
complete a form.	☐

3A | SHE OFTEN GOES TO AN ENGLISH LESSON

1 GRAMMAR
Position of adverbs of frequency

a Underline the correct words to complete the sentences.

1 I *catch usually* / *usually catch* the bus to school, and I *am always* / *always am* there by 7:30.
2 Moriko *sometimes watches* / *watches sometimes* TV after dinner, and she *often reads* / *reads often* a book before she goes to bed.
3 My father *goes always* / *always goes* to bed very early because he *is usually* / *usually is* tired by 10 o'clock.
4 I *often am* / *am often* at work before 9 o'clock, and I *don't finish usually* / *don't usually finish* work until 7 o'clock.

b Put the words in the correct order to make sentences. (Sometimes there is more than one possible answer.)

1 with their grandparents / lunch / usually / Sundays / they / have / on .
   They usually have lunch with their grandparents on Sundays.
2 always / on / am / I / after my fitness class / tired / Fridays .
   _____
3 at / work / my manager / 7:30 / starts / in the morning / often .
   _____
4 at weekends / together / never / dinner / has / his / family .
   _____
5 on Sundays / you / what time / do / go to bed / usually ?
   _____
6 gets / Pablo / sometimes / in his maths tests / 100% .
   _____

2 PRONUNCIATION
Sentence stress

a ▶ 03.01 Listen to the sentences and tick (✓) the correct stress markings.

1 a ✓ I <u>go</u> to the gym <u>twice</u> a <u>week</u>.
  b ☐ I go <u>to</u> the gym twice <u>a</u> week.
2 a ☐ <u>How</u> often <u>does</u> your brother <u>play</u> football?
  b ☐ How <u>often</u> does your brother play <u>football</u>?
3 a ☐ Caroline eats <u>fruit</u> <u>every</u> <u>day</u>.
  b ☐ <u>Caroline</u> eats fruit every <u>day</u>.
4 a ☐ Do they <u>often</u> go to the <u>Chinese</u> <u>restaurant</u>?
  b ☐ <u>Do</u> they often <u>go</u> to the <u>Chinese</u> restaurant?
5 a ☐ We go on holiday <u>three</u> times a <u>year</u>.
  b ☐ We <u>go</u> on holiday three times <u>a</u> year.
6 a ☐ My brother <u>never</u> does any <u>exercise</u>.
  b ☐ My brother never <u>does</u> any exercise.

3 VOCABULARY Time expressions

a Miguel has a very busy timetable. Use the information in the table to complete the sentences.

How often do you do these activities?	Mon	Tues	Wed	Thurs	Fri	Sat	Sun
1 go to school	✓	✓	✓	✓	✓	✓	
2 study maths		✓		✓			
3 play basketball	✓		✓			✓	
4 go swimming	✓	✓		✓			✓
5 watch TV	✓	✓	✓	✓	✓	✓	✓
6 visit your grandparents							✓
7 have band practice	✓		✓		✓		
8 work as a waiter in the café					✓	✓	

1 Miguel ___goes___ to school ___six times a___ week.
2 He _____ maths _____ week.
3 He _____ basketball _____ week.
4 He _____ swimming _____ week.
5 He _____ TV _____ day.
6 He _____ his grandparents _____ week.
7 He _____ band practice _____ week.
8 He _____ as a waiter in the café _____ week.

4 VOCABULARY Common verbs

a Complete the sentences with the verbs in the box.

buy   sells   find   decide   help
~~try~~   prefer   stay   cost   meet

1 Why don't we ___try___ the new café near the station?
2 When I go to Doha, I usually _____ with my friend, Tarek.
3 I _____ to go to the gym before I start work.
4 The new supermarket _____ Italian coffee. It's delicious!
5 I usually _____ a sandwich for lunch.
6 I don't like my job. I need to _____ a new one.
7 Can you _____ me carry the shopping?
8 I can't _____ which language to study – Spanish or Italian.
9 Why don't we _____ at the cinema at 7:15?
10 How much does a cup of tea _____ in the new café?

3B IMAGINE YOU HAVEN'T GOT THE INTERNET

1 GRAMMAR *have got*

a Underline the correct words to complete the sentences.

1 I *got* / *'ve got* / *'ve* a brilliant new smartphone. It *does have* / *have got* / *'s got* some amazing apps.

2 **A** *You have* / *Have you got* / *Do you got* the Internet on your TV?

B No, we *don't* / *haven't got* / *haven't*.

3 I *no have* / *don't got* / *haven't got* a digital camera, but I *'ve got* / *got* / *'ve* a camera on my phone.

4 My parents' car *hasn't got* / *haven't got* / *no has got* satnav, but they *got* / *'ve got* / *'s got* a good map.

5 She *got* / *'ve got* / *'s got* a fantastic new camera – it *'s got* / *have* / *got* 30 megapixels!

b Complete the conversation with the words in the box.

> 's got   have you   has   ~~have you got~~   've
> haven't   have they   they've got   it has   've got

ADAM ¹<u>Have you got</u> a computer?

SAM Yes, I have. I ²_____ got a laptop, but I ³_____ got a tablet.

ADAM What about your parents? ⁴_____ got a PC?

SAM No, they haven't, but ⁵_____ a tablet.

ADAM What other technology ⁶_____ and your family got?

SAM I ⁷_____ a smartphone and my sister ⁸_____ an amazing digital camera.

ADAM ⁹_____ your smartphone got any good apps on it?

SAM Yes, ¹⁰_____. It's got *Toktik*.

ADAM Really? I've got that app as well – it's brilliant!

2 VOCABULARY Technology

a Complete the crossword puzzle.

→ **Across**

5 You use <u>headphones</u> to listen to music on the bus.

7 I can take a photo of you with the _____ on my mobile phone.

8 If you want to see a paper copy of a document, you need to have a _____.

9 A _____ doesn't have a keyboard or a mouse. You only need to touch the screen.

10 You can use your _____ to call, text or email your friends. You can also use the Internet, play games and check maps.

↓ **Down**

1 A _____ is a small computer that you can carry with you.

2 When I want to listen to music with my friends, I connect my phone to a wireless _____.

3 I think the _____ on my laptop is very hard to use. It's really small and I've got big hands!

4 Some families have two or three _____ at home.

6 A _____ is a computer you wear on your wrist.

3 PRONUNCIATION Word stress

a ▶03.02 Listen and tick (✓) the words with the correct stress marking.

1	a	✓ comp<u>u</u>ter	b	☐ comput<u>er</u>
2	a	☐ head<u>phones</u>	b	☐ <u>head</u>phones
3	a	☐ <u>tab</u>let	b	☐ tab<u>let</u>
4	a	☐ <u>smart</u>watch	b	☐ smart<u>watch</u>
5	a	☐ key<u>board</u>	b	☐ <u>key</u>board
6	a	☐ <u>lap</u>top	b	☐ lap<u>top</u>
7	a	☐ c<u>a</u>mera	b	☐ cam<u>era</u>
8	a	☐ <u>print</u>er	b	☐ print<u>er</u>
9	a	☐ <u>speak</u>er	b	☐ spea<u>ker</u>
10	a	☐ smart<u>phone</u>	b	☐ <u>smart</u>phone

Crossword grid

5 across: H E A D P H O N E S

3C EVERYDAY ENGLISH
How about next Wednesday?

1 USEFUL LANGUAGE
Making arrangements

a Complete the conversation with the words in the box.

let me see	you free	don't you	fine	I can't
that'd be	how about	lovely idea	~~don't we~~	

CHRIS Why ¹ _don't we_ play tennis this weekend?
LUCY Tennis? Yeah, ² _____ great!
CHRIS ³ _____ on Sunday afternoon?
LUCY Mm, perhaps. ⁴ _____. Oh, I'm sorry,
⁵ _____. I usually visit my grandmother
on Sundays.
CHRIS Are ⁶ _____ on Saturday, then?
LUCY Yes, Saturday's ⁷ _____.
CHRIS Great. Why ⁸ _____ ask Tanya, too?
LUCY Yes, that's a ⁹ _____.

b ▶ 03.03 Listen and check.

c Put the conversation in the correct order.

☐	**LUKE**	Mm, perhaps. Let me see. No, I'm sorry, I can't.
1	**TOM**	Why don't we try that new Japanese restaurant this weekend?
☐	**TOM**	Why don't you bring your sister, too?
☐	**LUKE**	Yes, I'd love to. The question is when?
☐	**TOM**	OK, no problem. Are you free on Saturday?
☐	**LUKE**	I need to work late on Friday.
☐	**LUKE**	Sure. That's a really good idea.
☐	**TOM**	Great. See you on Saturday.
☐	**TOM**	Oh, that's a pity. Why not?
☐	**LUKE**	Yes, I am. Saturday's fine.
☐	**TOM**	How about on Friday?

d ▶ 03.04 Listen and check.

2 PRONUNCIATION Main stress

a ▶ 03.05 Listen and tick (✓) the stressed word in each sentence.

1 Why don't we go to the cinema?
  a ☐ go   b ✓ cinema
2 Yes, Monday's fine.
  a ☐ Monday's   b ☐ fine
3 Do you want to have a coffee after the lesson?
  a ☐ coffee   b ☐ lesson
4 Can I bring Leo?
  a ☐ bring   b ☐ Leo
5 Here's your coffee, Annie.
  a ☐ Here's   b ☐ coffee
6 Yes, I'd love to.
  a ☐ love   b ☐ to
7 That'd be great.
  a ☐ be   b ☐ great
8 Why don't we try it?
  a ☐ Why   b ☐ try

3D | SKILLS FOR WRITING
Can you join us?

1 READING

a Read the emails and tick (✓) the correct answers.

1 Luisa writes to Frida because she wants to …
- a ☐ tell Frida about her new flat in Los Angeles.
- b ☐ stay with Frida in Guadalajara.
- c ☐ invite Frida to come to Los Angeles for her birthday.
- d ☐ invite Frida to her wedding.

2 Frida can't come because …
- a ☐ she needs to work.
- b ☐ her mum wants to visit her.
- c ☐ her sister is getting married.
- d ☐ she is on holiday that weekend.

✉ 📝 ☆ ⚑   ⊗

Hi Frida,

How are things? I hope you like your new flat in Guadalajara.

It's my birthday next month and I'd like to spend it with my best friends. Would you like to come and stay with me in Los Angeles on 15 June? I've got a bedroom free at my house. I really hope you can come.

Love,

Luisa

✉ 📝 ☆ ⚑   ⊗

Hi Luisa,

It's lovely to hear from you and thanks very much for your invitation. I'd love to come, but I'm afraid I can't. I've got a family wedding (my sister, Eva) in Monterrey that weekend, so I can't come to Los Angeles. How about the weekend after?

Have a great birthday and hope to see you soon.

Love,

Frida

---

b Read the emails again. Underline the correct words to complete the sentences.

1 Frida lives in *Los Angeles / Monterrey / Guadalajara.*
2 Luisa's birthday is in *May / June / July.*
3 If she goes to Los Angeles, Frida can stay *in a hotel / with Luisa / with her sister.*
4 Frida's got a wedding in *Guadalajara / Los Angeles / Monterrey* when it's Luisa's birthday.
5 Frida would like to stay with Luisa on *15 June / 15 July / 22 June.*

2 WRITING SKILLS Inviting and replying

a Correct the mistakes in the conversation.

1 **MATEO** Hi, Clara. How you are?
   Hi, *Clara. How are you?*
2 **CLARA** Hello, Mateo. Fine, thanks. How you are?
3 **MATEO** Great, thank.
4 **CLARA** Good. By the way, it's my birthday next Saturday. Would you like to join for dinner at my house?
5 **MATEO** Yes, I love to. It would be great to see you, Gabriel and Sergio again.
6 **CLARA** Oh, good! And it's my graduation party on the 18th. Would you like come to that, too?
7 **MATEO** I'd love to, but I afraid I can't. I've got an important business trip to Bilbao that weekend and I can't change it.
8 **CLARA** Never mind. It no matter.
9 **MATEO** I hope you all to have a great time at the graduation party. See you on Saturday.
10 **CLARA** Yeah, I really looking forward to it. Bye!

b ▶ 03.06 Listen and check.

3 WRITING

a Choose an event and write an invitation to a friend or family member. Use the information in the box. Remember to:

- start and finish the invitation with a greeting and an ending (e.g., *Hello, Love, …*)
- ask how they are
- tell them where and when the event is
- talk about where they can stay
- say you hope they can come.

A Summer Pool Party
When: 23 July
Where: Your parents' house
Where people can stay:
Two bedrooms free

Housewarming Party*
When: 7 October
Where: Your new apartment
Where people can stay:
Small hotel in the town centre

*a party when you invite friends to your new home

b Now imagine you are your friend or family member. You can't go to the event. Write a reply and say why you can't go. Remember to:

- start and finish the reply with a greeting and an ending (e.g., *Hello, Love, …*)
- say thank you for the invitation
- say why you can't go
- say you hope the party goes well.

1 READING

a Read the text. Use the words in the box to complete the summary of the text.

---
end   friendly   friends   ~~magazine~~   often   questions

This is a page from a ^{1} _magazine_. First, it talks about ^{2}_____ and how important they are. Then there is a quiz. It asks ^{3}_____ about things you do. It wants to see how ^{4}_____ you are. It asks how ^{5}_____ you do different things. At the ^{6}_____, it tells you how friendly you are.

b Now answer the quiz. How friendly does it say you are?

c Write your own quiz with questions about how often people do things. It can be about anything you like – types of food people eat, what they do to keep fit, how they travel to work or school – anything you can think of! Here are some phrases you can use:

How often do you … ?
Once/twice a week
Once/twice a day
Three/four times a …

If you're so busy that you often forget about your friends, stop and think for a moment! Friends are very important. If you've got good friends, there is always someone to talk to, someone to laugh with and someone to help you with your problems. Life is more difficult for people who haven't got friends.

Remember that it's not easy to make friends! If you want friends, you need to be friendly. Don't always wait for your friends to call you. Make sure you call them sometimes, too. If someone invites you to their house, invite them to your house next time. If they have problems, try to help them.

We can't choose our families, but we can choose our friends. If you're not friendly, people may not choose you!

So how friendly are you?
Answer our quiz and find out!

HOW OFTEN DO YOU …

invite friends to your house?
a   more than once a week
b   once a week
c   less than once a week

chat with your friends on the Internet?
a   every day
b   once or twice a week
c   less than once a week

meet your friends (not at school or work)?
a   more than twice a week
b   once or twice a week
c   less than once a week

have parties?
a   three or four times a year or more
b   once or twice a year
c   less than once a year

send text messages to your friends?
a   at least once an hour
b   one to five times a day
c   less than once a day

go on holiday with friends?
a   once a year or more
b   less than once a year
c   never

Mostly "a" answers: You are very friendly. I want to be your friend! Make sure you leave time for work, too!

Mostly "b" answers: You have friends, but other things are important for you, too.

Mostly "c" answers: Your friends probably think you're not very interested in them. Try to be friendlier!

2 LISTENING

a ▶**03.07** Listen to the conversation. <u>Underline</u> the correct words to complete the sentences.

1 Lena *likes* / *doesn't like* gadgets.
2 Adam *wants* / *doesn't want* many gadgets.
3 Lena *wants* / *doesn't want* to explain to Adam why gadgets are useful.
4 Adam *wants* / *doesn't want* to meet Lena next week.

b Tick (✓) the gadgets mentioned in the conversation.

☐ computer   ☐ printer   ☐ keyboard
☐ headphones   ☐ smartphone   ☐ smartwatch
☐ laptop   ☐ tablet   ☐ smart speaker

c ▶**03.07** Listen to the conversation again. Tick (✓) the correct answers.

1 What does Lena show Adam at the beginning of their conversation?
   a ☐ a smartphone
   b ☑ a smart speaker
   c ☐ a tablet
2 What does Lena say she often uses her smart speaker for?
   a ☐ asking questions
   b ☐ online shopping
   c ☐ listening to music
3 Why does Adam say he needs a laptop?
   a ☐ to look at photos
   b ☐ for his studies
   c ☐ to play games
4 Why does Lena invite Adam for a coffee?
   a ☐ to show him her smartphone
   b ☐ to look at smart speakers online
   c ☐ to fix his laptop
5 When do Lena and Adam decide to meet?
   a ☐ next Monday
   b ☐ next month
   c ☐ next Friday
6 What does Lena say she can use to find the café?
   a ☐ her smartphone
   b ☐ her laptop
   c ☐ her smart speaker

d Write about the gadgets you have got and how you use them. Think about these questions:

• Which ones have you got? What do you use them for? Do you like them?
• Which ones haven't you got? Why not? Would you like to have any of them?

1 GRAMMAR

Correct the sentences. (Sometimes there is more than one possible answer.)

1 My car have got new speakers.
   My car has got new speakers.
2 Look, I got the latest smartphone!
3 She haven't got a good camera on her phone.
4 Do you got a laptop in your bag?
5 **A** Have they got apps on their phones?
   B Yes, they got.
6 We got a lot of friends in Pakistan.
7 **A** Has Lien got a big family?
   B No, she don't.
8 He got a new computer now.

2 VOCABULARY

Correct the sentences.

1 I usually go to football training one time a week.
   I usually go to football training once a week.
2 They go swimming everyday.
3 We study English three times the week.
4 My friends and I usually go to the cinema about two times a month.
5 My sister goes to the gym once on the week.
6 My wife and I go on holiday three times at the year.

3 WORDPOWER Prepositions of time

<u>Underline</u> the correct words to complete the sentences.
1 He usually finishes work *in* / *on* / <u>*at*</u> 6 o'clock.
2 Silawan's birthday is *on* / *in* / *at* April.
3 *At* / *In* / *On* the evening they sometimes watch TV.
4 The River Volga in Russia always freezes *in* / *on* / *at* the winter.
5 My parents often play tennis *at* / *on* / *in* Sundays.
6 *On* / *At* / *In* weekends I usually get up late.
7 That restaurant closes *at* / *in* / *on* midnight.
8 At my school, the first class starts *in* / *at* / *on* 8 o'clock.

↻ REVIEW YOUR PROGRESS

Look again at Review your progress on p. 38 of the Student's Book. How well can you do these things now?
3 = very well   2 = well   1 = not so well

I CAN ...	
talk about routines	☐
talk about technology in my life	☐
make arrangements	☐
write an informal invitation.	☐

4A | TRY SOME INTERESTING FOOD

1 GRAMMAR
Countable and uncountable nouns; *a / an*, *some*, *any*

a <u>Underline</u> the correct words to complete the sentences.

1 I need some <u>*bread*</u> / *breads* to make sandwiches.
2 Excuse me. Have you got any *carrot* / *carrots*?
3 The *pastas are* / *pasta is* really good in this restaurant.
4 I'd like *some lamb* / *a lamb*, please.
5 The *fruits are* / *fruit is* really fresh in this market.
6 You can buy fantastic *cheese* / *cheeses* in this market.
7 I love Mexican *food* / *foods* – I think it's the best in the world.
8 Can you buy me some *milks* / *milk* from the supermarket?

b <u>Underline</u> the correct words to complete the conversation. (Sometimes there is more than one possible answer.)

TIM We can make ¹*any* / *a* / <u>*some*</u> sandwiches for lunch.
RACHEL Good idea. Have we got ²*any* / *some* / *a* bread?
TIM Yes, we have. We've got ³*any* / *some* / *a* really fresh bread. It's still warm!
RACHEL OK. Have we got ⁴*any* / *some* / *a* turkey or chicken to put in it?
TIM Um, let me see. We haven't got ⁵*some* / *a* / *any* turkey, but we have ⁶*some* / *a* / *any* chicken.
RACHEL Have we got ⁷*a* / *some* / *any* cheese in the fridge?
TIM Yes, we've got ⁸*some* / *a* / *any* French cheese and ⁹*any* / *a* / *some* Swiss cheese.
RACHEL OK. And what about vegetables? Have we got ¹⁰*a* / *any* / *some*?
TIM Yes, we've got ¹¹*a* / *some* / *any* mushrooms, and there's ¹²*a* / *any* / *some* big tomato. But I'm afraid we haven't got ¹³*a* / *some* / *any* onions.
RACHEL OK. I can make ¹⁴*some* / *a* / *any* cheese and tomato sandwich or ¹⁵*a* / *any* / *some* chicken sandwich.

2 VOCABULARY Food

a Match the pictures with the words in the box.

crisps   salad   pear   lemon   melon   garlic
burger   grapes   ~~chicken~~   cereal

b Complete the table with the words in the box.

~~chicken~~   steak   grape   carrot   mushroom   burger
melon   onion   pear   lamb   lemon   garlic

Meat	Vegetables	Fruit
chicken		

3 PRONUNCIATION
Sound and spelling: *ea*

a ▶ 04.01 Listen and complete the table with the words in the box.

~~see~~   hair   meat   pair   great   parent   say   bear
need   date   meet   hate   air   play   sheep

/eɪ/ (e.g., st**ea**k)	/iː/ (e.g., b**ea**n)	/eə/ (e.g., p**ea**r)
	see	

1   <u>chicken</u>

2 _____

3 _____

4 _____

5 _____

6 _____

7 _____

8 _____

9 _____

10 _____

4B HOW MUCH CHOCOLATE?

1 GRAMMAR
Quantifiers: *much, many, a lot (of)*

a Put the words in the correct order to make sentences.

1 need / oranges / we / how / do / many ?
How many oranges do we need?

2 drinks / a / milk / of / she / lot .
_____

3 haven't / much / sorry / got / money / I'm / I .
_____

4 eat / brother / many / little / my / vegetables / doesn't .
_____

5 day / you / fruit / every / do / much / eat / how ?
_____

6 a / recipe / butter / need / for / little / this / we .
_____

7 in / don't / afternoon / I / coffee / usually / the / much / drink .
_____

8 few / for / can / tomatoes / you / a / buy / salad / the ?
_____

b Complete the conversation with the words in the box.

many	much	a lot (x2)	a few	lot of
~~how much~~	a little	how many		

LUCA Hi, Nadia. I'm at the supermarket, but I forgot the shopping list. What do I need to buy?

NADIA Ha ha! No problem. I've got the list here.

LUCA [1]*How much* milk do we need?

NADIA We need [2]_____ . Can you get two litres, please?

LUCA All right. And [3]_____ eggs?

NADIA Just [4]_____ . Just buy one box of six.

LUCA OK. Do we need [5]_____ vegetables?

NADIA Yes, we do. Buy a [6]_____ vegetables. You know my mother's a vegetarian!

LUCA And do we need [7]_____ cheese?

NADIA No, we've still got quite [8]_____ in the fridge, so don't buy any.

LUCA What about rice?

NADIA We've only got [9]_____ rice at home, so get one big bag.

LUCA OK, no problem.

NADIA Right, I think that's everything. Thanks for going to the supermarket!

2 VOCABULARY Cooking

a Complete the food phrases with the words in the box.

roasted	jar	fried	bar	~~bag~~	packet	bottle	grilled

1 a ___*bag*___ of rice   2 _____ chicken

3 _____ fish   4 _____ eggs

5 a _____ of jam   6 a _____ of chocolate

7 a _____ of biscuits   8 a _____ of water

b ▶04.02 Listen and complete the sentences.

1 I'd like ___*boiled*___ potatoes, please.
2 I'd like _____ fish, please.
3 I'd like _____ vegetables, please.
4 I'd like a _____ egg, please.
5 I'd like a _____ of cola, please.
6 I'd like a _____ of soup, please.
7 I'd like a _____ of tomatoes, please.
8 I'd like a _____ of crisps, please.

4C EVERYDAY ENGLISH
Do we need a reservation?

1 USEFUL LANGUAGE
Arriving at and ordering a meal in a restaurant

a Complete the conversation with the words in the box.

maybe not   on the left   the name   can we have
this way   those two   prefer   ~~reservation~~   for six   the one

WAITRESS   Good evening. Do you have a ¹ _reservation_ ?
PAUL   Yes, we have a reservation ² _____ people.
WAITRESS   Certainly. What's ³ _____ ?
PAUL   Henderson.
WAITRESS   Yes, that's fine.
PAUL   ⁴ _____ a table outside, please?
WAITRESS   Yes, of course. ⁵ _____ , please.
      ⁶ _____ over there are both free.
PAUL   What do you think? ⁷ _____ on the right?
JENNY   I'm not sure. What about the one ⁸ _____ ?
PAUL   If you ⁹ _____ . It's your birthday.
JENNY   Well, ¹⁰ _____ . This one's fine.

b ▶ 04.03 Listen and check.

c Tick (✓) the correct sentences in the conversation. Correct the other sentences. (Sometimes there is more than one possible answer.)

1. ☐ **A** You are ready to order?
   Are you ready to order?
2. ☐ **B** Yes, I think so.
3. ☐ **A** What do you like for your starter?
4. ☐ **B** I like the mixed bean salad, please.
5. ☐ **A** And for your main course?
6. ☐ **B** I take the chicken curry.
7. ☐ **A** You like chips with that?
8. ☐ **B** Yes, please.
9. ☐ **A** And in your starter, madam?
10. ☐ **C** I have the fried fish, please.
11. ☐ **A** Fried fish in lemon sauce.
12. ☐ **C** Then I'd have the steak. No, wait. I'll have the spaghetti.
13. ☐ **B** Oh, that's a good idea. Can I change my menu?
14. ☐ **A** Yes, of course.
15. ☐ **B** I'll eat the same. Spaghetti with meatballs for my main.

d ▶ 04.04 Listen and check.

2 PRONUNCIATION   Word groups

a Match the phrases in the box to make sentences that people use in a restaurant.

Where would you like to sit
or do you need some more time?
~~and then the steak.~~
– inside or outside?
I'll have the soup,
with some rice.
Can we have a table for four
~~I'd like the chicken salad~~
by the window if possible?
Would you like to order now
and the spaghetti for my main.
I'd like the lamb curry

Word group 1	Word group 2
1 _I'd like the chicken salad_	_and then the steak._
2 _____	_____
3 _____	_____
4 _____	_____
5 _____	_____
6 _____	_____

b ▶ 04.05 Listen and check.

c ▶ 04.06 Listen to the sentences and tick (✓) the stressed words.

1. I'd like the chicken curry, please.
   a. ☐ chicken
   b. ✓ curry
2. Can we have a table by the window if possible?
   a. ☐ table
   b. ☐ window
3. I'd like the mushroom soup for my starter.
   a. ☐ mushroom soup
   b. ☐ starter
4. Would you like to order now?
   a. ☐ order
   b. ☐ now
5. I'll have the spaghetti for my main.
   a. ☐ spaghetti
   b. ☐ main
6. Where would you like to sit – outside?
   a. ☐ sit
   b. ☐ outside

4D SKILLS FOR WRITING
Next, decide on your menu

1 READING

a Read the recipe for Niçoise salad and tick (✓) the correct answer.

1 ☐ This dish is for people who like a lot of meat.
2 ☐ This dish is for people who don't eat any meat or fish.
3 ☐ This dish is for people who like fish, vegetables and eggs.
4 ☐ This dish is for people who don't like many vegetables.

b Read the recipe again. Are the sentences true (*T*) or false (*F*)?

1 You need to use fresh fish for this salad.
2 It takes less than an hour to make this salad.
3 You can add the eggs, potatoes and beans to the salad when they're warm.
4 You put all the food together on the same plate.
5 You add the dressing last.

2 WRITING SKILLS
Making the order clear

a Read the recipe for a perfect Spanish omelette. Put the instructions in the correct order.

Spanish omelette

Preparation time: about 45 minutes

Ingredients: For this recipe, you need six eggs, a large onion, 500 grams of potatoes, olive oil, salt and pepper.

Instructions:

☐ Next, cook all the ingredients together for about 10 minutes.

☐ Then, fry the onions and potatoes in the olive oil for 30 minutes, or until the potatoes are soft.

☐ Finally, turn the omelette over and cook for 5 more minutes.

☐ After that, put the onions and potatoes into a large bowl with the eggs, salt and pepper and mix everything together.

☑ 1 First, cut the onion and potatoes into small pieces.

Niçoise Salad

Preparation time:
45 minutes

Ingredients:
For this recipe, you need some fresh tuna fish (or a can of tuna), some potatoes, some tomatoes, some green beans, a large lettuce, an onion, four eggs and some black olives.

Instructions:

1 First, boil the eggs, potatoes and green beans. Then, put them in the fridge until they are cold.

2 Next, wash the lettuce and tomatoes and cut the onion into small pieces.

3 After that, put the lettuce on a large plate with the tuna, tomatoes, onion, potatoes, beans and olives.

4 Finally, make a dressing with olive oil, vinegar and mustard. Put it on the salad and mix everything together.

3 WRITING

a Look at the pictures of someone making a pizza. Use the information under the pictures to complete the recipe. Add your favourite pizza toppings. Remember to make the order clear (e.g., *First, After that, …*).

1 Mix: flour, water, oil 　　2 Make: pizza base 　　3 Put on: tomato sauce, cheese

4 Add: toppings (e.g., mushrooms, peppers …) 　　5 Bake: 10 minutes

A _____ Pizza

Preparation time: _____
Ingredients: _____
Instructions:
First, _____
_____
_____
_____
_____
_____

1 READING

a Read the magazine article. Complete each sentence with the correct paragraph number.

a Paragraph __4__ talks about the fruit Rob grows.

b Paragraph ____ talks about how healthy it is to eat fruit and vegetables.

c Paragraph ____ talks about the vegetables Rob grows.

d Paragraph ____ talks about how good it is for children to see how we grow food.

e Paragraph ____ gives reasons to grow your own food.

b Read the article again. Are the sentences true (*T*) or false (*F*)?

1 It is expensive to grow your own vegetables.

2 You don't need a lot of space to grow a few vegetables.

3 Rob Green doesn't like growing vegetables because it's hard work.

4 He thinks his vegetables are better than the vegetables in the supermarkets.

5 He gets apples and oranges from his trees.

6 He cooks the apples he grows.

7 His children eat a lot of the strawberries.

8 His children think that vegetables always come from the supermarket.

c Write about the fruit and vegetables you eat. Think about these questions:

- What types of fruit and vegetables do you eat most often?
- What are your favourite vegetables?
- What is your favourite fruit?
- Do you think fruit and vegetables are expensive?
- Where do you get them from?
- Do you grow any fruit or vegetables (or do you know anyone who does)?

Are fresh fruit and vegetables too expensive?
Why not grow your own?

1 We all know that it's good for us to eat a lot of fresh fruit and vegetables. But it can be expensive, especially if you have a big family.

2 Why not grow your own? It's cheap, it's easy and it's fun! You don't even need much space. A box in the window is enough to grow some salad.

3 Rob Green has a vegetable garden at his house in Norwich. He says, 'It can be hard work sometimes, but I love it. I grow a lot of different vegetables, for example, carrots, onions and beans. It saves me a lot of money, and the vegetables I grow are better than anything you can buy in the supermarkets.'

4 His garden has an apple tree and a pear tree. The apples aren't very sweet, but he bakes them with brown sugar, and the family eat them for dessert with ice cream. Rob also grows strawberries, and he usually makes a few jars of jam each summer. 'I'd like to make more,' he says. 'The only problem is that, after the children see the strawberries, there aren't many left!'

5 Rob often cooks with his children, and he says that it's good for them to see where their food comes from, too. 'Children need to know that food doesn't arrive at the supermarkets in packets.'

2 LISTENING

a ▶ 04.07 Listen to the conversation. Tick (✓) the correct words to complete the sentences.

1 Evie and Ethan can't go out because …
  a ✓ of the snow.
  b ☐ they don't know where the supermarket is.
  c ☐ Ethan wants to stay at home and eat.
2 Ethan is worried because …
  a ☐ he doesn't like bread.
  b ☐ he doesn't know how to cook.
  c ☐ they haven't got much food.
3 Evie's not worried because …
  a ☐ she likes burgers.
  b ☐ she thinks she can cook a meal.
  c ☐ she wants to go out for a meal.
4 Evie's meal is very unusual because …
  a ☐ she only uses food she finds in the kitchen.
  b ☐ she likes making unusual food.
  c ☐ she only makes one dish.

b Complete the table with the words in the box.

~~bread~~ eggs carrots cheese chocolate
crisps jam onions pasta rice yoghurt

Evie and Ethan have …	Evie and Ethan haven't got …
bread	

c ▶ 04.07 Listen to the conversation again. Put the sentences in the order they happen.

☐ Ethan doesn't like the sandwiches very much.
☐ Ethan doesn't think they can make a meal from the food they find.
☐ For their starter, they have rice and cheese soup.
1 Evie and Ethan have to stay inside because of the snow.
☐ Evie and Ethan look in their kitchen to see what food they have.
☐ For their main course, they have fried onions with carrot sandwiches.
☐ Evie says she will make a meal for them.
☐ For dessert, they have boiled pasta and chocolate sauce.

d Think about the food in *your* kitchen. Write about an unusual meal you can make with the food you have. Use *much*, *a lot*, *many* and *a little* to say how much of each food there is.

◉ Review and extension

1 GRAMMAR

Correct the sentences.

1 I'd like any potatoes and any carrots, please.
  I'd like some potatoes and some carrots, please.
2 I'm sorry, I haven't got a butter this week.
3 Can I have some bag of rice, please?
4 Yes, we've got any eggs in the fridge.
5 Can you buy a bread at the supermarket?
6 No, there aren't some mushrooms in the fridge.
7 We need a onion for the salad.
8 Have we got a milk?

2 VOCABULARY

Correct the sentences.

1 Can I have roast kitchen and boiled potatoes, please?
  Can I have roast chicken and boiled potatoes, please?
2 For my starter, I'd like the mushroom soap.
3 Would you like braed with your salad?
4 I'll have lam curry and rice for my main course.
5 Would you like some vedgetables with your steak?
6 I usually have serial with milk in the morning.
7 Do you eat yoghurt with frute? It's delicious!
8 Would you like a cheese sanwhich?

3 WORDPOWER *like*

Match questions 1–6 with answers a–f.

1 [d] Would you like to go for a coffee?
2 ☐ What type of food do you like?
3 ☐ What would you like?
4 ☐ What's your sister like?
5 ☐ What kind of music does she like?
6 ☐ Is your sister like you?

a Yes, she is. We're both very tall.
b She likes rock, pop and jazz.
c She's friendly and very popular.
d Yes, I'd love to.
e I like Italian food.
f I'd like a pizza, please.

◔ REVIEW YOUR PROGRESS

Look again at Review your progress on p. 48 of the Student's Book. How well can you do these things now?
3 = very well   2 = well   1 = not so well

I CAN …	
talk about the food I want	☐
talk about the food I eat every day	☐
arrive at and order a meal in a restaurant	☐
write a blog post about something I know how to do.	☐

5A | THERE AREN'T ANY PARKS OR SQUARES

1 GRAMMAR *there is / there are*

a Underline the correct words to complete the conversation.

A ¹*Is there / Are there / There is* any good places to go in the evening?

B Yes, ²*there is / it is / there are.* ³*There is / There's / There are* some dance clubs and cafés.

A ⁴*There is / Are there / Is there* any good restaurants?

B Yes, ⁵*there are / there's / there is.* ⁶*There are / There's / It's* a fantastic Italian restaurant in the town square.

A ⁷*There is / There are / Is there* a theatre?

B No, ⁸*there is / there isn't / there aren't,* but ⁹*there are / there's / there isn't* one in Weston.

A What about interesting places to visit?

B Well, ¹⁰*there's / there are / is there* an old castle, but ¹¹*there isn't / there are / there aren't* any museums or art galleries.

A ¹²*Are there / Is there / There is* a metro?

B No, but we have a good bus system.

b Put the words in the correct order to make sentences.

1 **A** your town / there / in / nice restaurants / are / any ?
   Are there any nice restaurants in your town?
   B there / yes, / are .
   _____

2 **A** the / beautiful park / in / there / town centre / is / a ?
   _____
   B is / yes, / there .
   _____

3 near / there / metro station / a / isn't / my house .
   _____

4 near / shops / any / there / my office / aren't .
   _____

5 the station / there / near / cheap hotels / are / some .
   _____

6 the river / there's / near / new café / a .
   _____

7 **A** city centre / any / in / there / are / the / interesting buildings ?
   _____
   B aren't / no, / there .
   _____

2 VOCABULARY Places in a city

a Write the names of the places in a city under the pictures.

1 ____concert hall____

2 _____

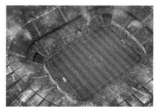

3 _____

4 _____

5 _____

6 _____

b Complete the sentences with the words in the box.

> street   post office   sports centre   buildings
> police station   theatre   stadium   ~~restaurant~~

1 The pizzas at the new Italian __restaurant__ are really good!
2 They've got Shakespeare's *Romeo and Juliet* at our local _____.
3 There are a lot of houses in my _____, and there are also a few shops and cafés.
4 There's a football match at the _____.
5 You can buy stamps for your postcards at the _____.
6 There are a lot of beautiful _____ in our town. The concert hall and museum are amazing!
7 There is a fantastic pool at our _____.
8 If someone takes your mobile phone, you need to go to the _____.

3 PRONUNCIATION
Sound and spelling: /b/ and /p/

a ▶05.01 Listen and underline the correct words.

1 bit / pit
2 put / but
3 buy / pie
4 bear / pear
5 part / Bart
6 be / pea

5B | WHOSE WARDROBE IS THAT?

1 GRAMMAR Possessive pronouns and possessive 's

a Choose the correct words to complete the sentences.

1 This isn't *Muneers' car* / *the Muneer car* / *Muneer's car*. It's *my* / *mine* / *the mine*.
2 *Our* / *Ours* / *The our* parents live in the centre of Pattaya.
3 No, this isn't *the my* / *my* / *mine* dog. It's *their* / *theirs* / *they're*.
4 Sarah is *Matthew's sister* / *the sister Matthew* / *Matthews sister*. *Her* / *Hers* / *His* boyfriend's Nigerian.
5 *Who's* / *Whose* / *Who* phone is this? Is it *the your* / *your* / *yours*?
6 *Kenji and Yuka* / *The Kenji and Yuka'* / *Kenji and Yuka's* flat has got two large bedrooms.

b Find the mistakes in the words in **bold** and rewrite the sentences.

1 **A Who's** apartment is this?
   Whose apartment is this?
   B It's **Monicas**.
   _____

2 **Its** got a living room, two bedrooms and **theirs** a small kitchen.
   _____

3 **Hers** sister, Cristina, lives with her. **Their** identical twins.
   _____

4 They've got a cat, but **its** not **there's**. **Its** their **brothers** cat. **It's** name's Brandy.
   _____

5 **Monicas** bedroom is quite large, but **Cristinas'** bedroom is very small.
   _____

6 **A Who's** is the furniture?
   _____
   B Monica says that the sofa is **her**, but Cristina says **its** their **brother**.

7 **There** brother's got a new car. **Its** really fast!
   _____

2 VOCABULARY Furniture

a Complete the crossword puzzle with the words in the box.

> armchair   bedside table   bookcase   chest of drawers
> cooker   cupboard   curtains   lamp   mirror   sink   sofa
> wardrobe   washing machine

→ Across

3 You use a __washing__ __machine__ to wash your clothes.
6 You need to turn the _____ on when it gets dark.
7 You can put all of your books on that _____ in the living room.
8 The large plates are in that _____ in the kitchen.
9 Is there a _____ in the kitchen so I can make my dinner?
10 Three people can sit on that big _____ to watch TV.
11 Why don't you put your jackets, shirts and trousers in this _____ and not on the floor?
12 You can wash the plates and cups in the _____.

↓ Down

1 I always look in the _____ when I brush my hair.
2 I have a clock on the _____ _____ next to my bed.
4 My grandfather always sits in his favourite _____.
5 Put your sweaters, T-shirts and socks in the _____ _____ _____ in your bedroom.
8 At night, close your _____ before you go to bed.

[Crossword grid: 3 Across reads W A S H I N G M A C H I N E, with numbered cells 1, 2, 4, 5, 6, 7, 8, 9, 10, 11, 12]

3 PRONUNCIATION
Sound and spelling: vowels before *r*

a ▶ 05.02 Look at the words and listen to the pronunciation of the letters in **bold**. Complete the table with the words in the box.

> b**o**x   furniture   hard   lamp   curtains   test   door
> sink   armchair   president   wardrobe   mad

1 Short sounds (e.g., am)	2 Long sounds (e.g., arm)
box	

5C EVERYDAY ENGLISH
Is there a bank near here?

1 USEFUL LANGUAGE
Asking for and giving directions

a Put the conversation in the correct order.

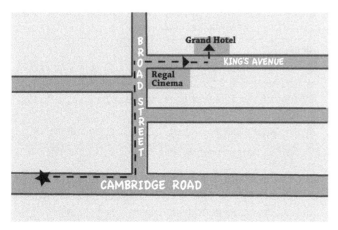

☐ So, straight on, then turn left into Broad Street?

☐ Yes, then go along King's Avenue for about 100 metres. The hotel is on your left.

[1] Excuse me. Can you tell me the way to the Grand Hotel, please?

☐ Yes, that's right. Then go straight along Broad Street until you come to the Regal Cinema. Then turn right into King's Avenue.

☐ Great. Thanks very much.

☐ Yes, of course. Go straight on for about 200 metres, then turn left into Broad Street.

☐ So, that's right into King's Avenue after the cinema?

b ▶ 05.03 Listen and check.

c Put the words in the correct order to make sentences.

1 until / go / on / you come / on / straight / your / to / a metro station / left .
   Go straight on until you come to a metro station
   on your left.

2 turn left / and go along / the cinema / at / for 250 metres / Huntingdon Road .
   _____
   _____

3 please / you / can / how / get / us / tell / to / the station / to ?
   _____
   _____

4 along / for 100 metres, / go / and / the High Street / right / your / the concert hall / is / on .
   _____
   _____

5 is / stop / a / here / bus / near / there ?
   _____
   _____

6 straight / for 250 metres, / on / right / then turn / so / Park Street / into ?
   _____

7 it's / the / corner / That's right. / next / on / the bank / to .
   _____

8 I / to / Excuse me. / do / the train station / how / from here / get ?
   _____
   _____

d ▶ 05.04 Listen and check.

2 PRONUNCIATION Sentence stress

a ▶ 05.05 Listen and tick (✓) the stressed word in each sentence.

1 Go along Acacia Road.
   a ☐ go
   b ✓ along

2 Go straight on until you come to the hospital.
   a ☐ come
   b ☐ hospital

3 Can you tell me how to get to the swimming pool, please?
   a ☐ swimming pool
   b ☐ please

4 Go straight on for about 200 metres.
   a ☐ go
   b ☐ straight

5 Turn right into Carlisle Avenue.
   a ☐ turn
   b ☐ right

6 The sports centre is on the left.
   a ☐ on
   b ☐ left

7 Is there a bank near here?
   a ☐ bank
   b ☐ here

8 Go straight on for about 200 metres.
   a ☐ 200
   b ☐ metres

6B | I PLAYED ANYTHING AND EVERYTHING

1 GRAMMAR Past simple: positive

a Complete the text with the simple past forms of the verbs in brackets.

Stan Lee ¹_____ (be) an American comic book writer. He ²_____ (be born) in 1922 in New York City. He ³_____ (have) one younger brother, Larry. As a boy, Lee ⁴_____ (like) writing. In high school, he ⁵_____ (enter) a weekly writing competition by a popular newspaper. Lee ⁶_____ (win) the competition three weeks in a row. The newspaper ⁷_____ (tell) him to become a professional writer. In 1942, Lee ⁸_____ (join) the US Army. While in the army, Lee ⁹_____ (write) one story a week for a comic book company. In the 1960s, Lee ¹⁰_____ (help) create the Fantastic Four for Marvel Comics. The characters ¹¹_____ (be) so popular that Marvel Comics ¹²_____ (ask) Lee to help create more characters and stories. Lee ¹³_____ (become) famous for helping to create such characters as the Hulk, Thor, Iron Man, the X-Men, Daredevil, Doctor Strange and Spider-Man. Lee ¹⁴_____ (die) on November 12, 2018. He ¹⁵_____ (receive) many awards during his lifetime.

b Underline the correct words to complete the sentences.

1 Ilyas *meeted* / *met* / *metted* Leyla when they *were* / *was* / *been* at university together.
2 The taxi *stopped* / *stoped* / *stopt* in front of the station, and she *gived* / *gaved* / *gave* the driver €20.
3 He *were* / *was* / *am* born in 1942 and *died* / *die* / *dyed* in 2021.
4 When they *find* / *finded* / *found* the backpack in the park, they *taked* / *took* / *taken* it to the police station.
5 Last year, my brother *goed* / *was* / *went* to Las Vegas on holiday. It's a really expensive place to visit. He *spent* / *spended* / *spented* over $2,000 in three days!
6 My mother *maked* / *maid* / *made* a big birthday cake for my brother yesterday, and we *eated* / *ate* / *ated* three pieces each!
7 My sister *playd* / *plaied* / *played* the piano very well when she was eight, and my parents *bought* / *buyed* / *buied* her a guitar when she was fifteen.
8 Supattra *workt* / *worked* / *walked* hard at university and then *getted* / *gotted* / *got* a fantastic job in Bangkok.

2 VOCABULARY
Past simple: irregular verbs

a Complete the sentences with the past simple forms of the verbs in the box.

go ~~eat~~ give read bring buy
think ~~make~~ have cost get come

1 Last night, she ___*made*___ us a lovely chicken soup. Sorry, there isn't any for you today because we ___*ate*___ it all.
2 My uncle _____ a car last week. It _____ £8,000.
3 We _____ to an Italian restaurant last night and _____ some fantastic dishes!
4 She _____ to my house for dinner on Saturday and _____ her new boyfriend with her.
5 I _____ that new book about Leonardo da Vinci over the weekend. I _____ it was really interesting.
6 I _____ some nice chocolates for my birthday. My friend Alison _____ them to me.

3 PRONUNCIATION -ed endings

a ▶06.03 Listen to the past simple verbs. Do they have an extra syllable? Tick (✓) the correct box.

	No extra syllable: /t/ or /d/	Extra syllable: /ɪd/
1 closed	✓	
2 waited		
3 decided		
4 arrived		
5 loved		
6 studied		
7 visited		
8 opened		
9 started		
10 worked		

6C EVERYDAY ENGLISH
Can you call me back?

1 USEFUL LANGUAGE
Leaving a voicemail message and asking for someone on the phone

a Complete the conversation with the words in the box.

> a minute   Ian's phone   ~~leave~~   isn't here   back soon
> there   it's   can he   ~~right now~~   on my mobile
> I'll tell   ~~this is~~   it's me   call me back

CONVERSATION 1

IAN   Hello, ¹___this is___ Ian Smith. I'm not here ²___right now___. Please ³___leave___ a message after the tone.

ABBY   Hi, Ian. Can you ⁴_____? You can call me on my work number or ⁵_____.

CONVERSATION 2

DAVID   Hello. ⁶_____.

ABBY   Oh, hello. Is Ian ⁷_____, please?

DAVID   Sorry, he ⁸_____ just now. He's in a meeting.

ABBY   That's OK. ⁹_____ his sister, Abby. ¹⁰_____ call me back?

DAVID   OK, ¹¹_____ him. He'll be ¹²_____. Oh, just ¹³_____. Here he comes now … Ian, it's Abby.

IAN   Hi, Abby. ¹⁴_____.

ABBY   Hello, Ian. At last!

b ▶ 06.04 Listen and check.

c Put the words in the correct order to make sentences.

1 after / leave / please / the tone / a message .
   Please leave a message after the tone.

2 this afternoon / back / can you / call me ?
   _____

3 can / wait / you / a minute ?
   _____

4 or my mobile / call me / on my / you can / home phone .
   _____

5 right now / I'm not / here .
   _____

6 here / just now / sorry, / she isn't .
   _____

d ▶ 06.05 Listen and check.

2 PRONUNCIATION
Sound and spelling: *a*

a ▶ 06.06 Listen to the words with the *a* sounds in **bold**. Then complete the table with the words in the box.

> ~~f**a**ll~~   d**a**te   cott**a**ge   **a**m   c**a**ke   l**a**nguage   dr**a**w   h**a**ppy
> w**a**lk   S**a**turd**a**y   man**a**ge   em**a**il   b**a**ll   m**a**n   n**a**me

/æ/ (e.g., *thanks*)	/ɔː/ (e.g., *call*)	/ɪ/ (e.g., *message*)	/eɪ/ (e.g., *later*)
	fall		

6D SKILLS FOR WRITING
Five months later, we got married

1 READING

a Read about Marco Morales and tick (✓) the one wrong answer.

1. ☐ Marco wasn't born in the USA.
2. ☐ His wife's name is Ruby.
3. ☐ He has two children.
4. ☐ They live in Arizona.

Marco was born in El Salvador in 1978. When he was four years old, his family moved to Arizona in the USA because his father got a job as an engineer in Phoenix. Marco went to school in Scottsdale. He left school in 1996 and went to university in Florida. He studied Economics there. He graduated from university in 2000 and got his first job with a big bank in Miami. In 2005, he met Ruby, and they got married in 2009. Six years later, their first child, Mason, was born. In 2016, Marco and Ruby moved to Mexico City. Marco became the vice-president of a bank there, and Ruby got a job as a teacher at an international school. Their daughter, Lydia, was born in 2017.

b Read about Marco Morales again. Are the sentences true (*T*) or false (*F*)?

1. Marco's family moved to Arizona in 1982.
2. He left school when he was sixteen years old.
3. His first job was in a bank in Memphis.
4. Mason was born in 2015.
5. In 2016, Marco and his family left the USA.

2 WRITING SKILLS
Linking ideas in the past

a Complete the paragraph with the words in the box. Use Sara's timeline to help you.

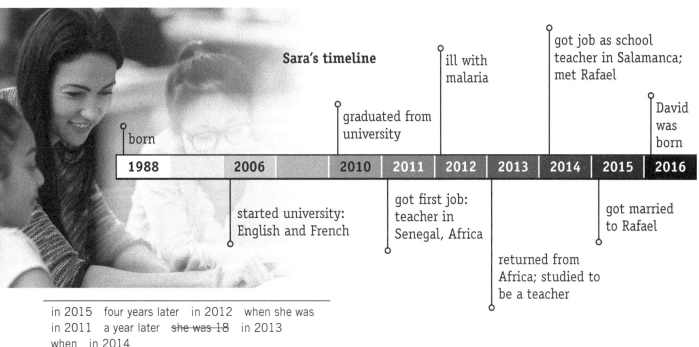

Sara's timeline

born	started university: English and French	graduated from university	got first job: teacher in Senegal, Africa	ill with malaria	returned from Africa; studied to be a teacher	got job as school teacher in Salamanca; met Rafael	got married to Rafael	David was born
1988	2006	2010	2011	2012	2013	2014	2015	2016

in 2015   four years later   in 2012   when she was
in 2011   a year later   ~~she was 18~~   in 2013
when   in 2014

Sara was born in Pamplona in 1988. When ¹ _she was 18_, Sara went to university in Valencia, where she studied English and French. ² _____ she graduated from university, and ³ _____ she got her first job in Africa. ⁴ _____ in Senegal, she worked as an English teacher. ⁵ _____ she was ill with malaria for three months. ⁶ _____ she returned to Spain and went back to university to become a teacher. ⁷ _____ she got a job at a school in Salamanca. ⁸ _____ she was in Salamanca, she met her husband, Rafael. ⁹ _____ they got married, and ¹⁰ _____ their first child, David, was born.

3 WRITING

a Write the life story of a famous person. Use linking phrases in the story. Think about:

- when/where they were born
- where/what they studied
- what jobs they did in the past and now
- where they lived in the past and now
- their family (parents, husband/wife, children).

UNIT 6
Reading and listening extension

1 READING

a Read about Nina and her family. Complete each sentence with the correct paragraph number.

1 Paragraph ⎯5⎯ talks about the good idea Nina's mum had.
2 Paragraph ⎯⎯ says that her grandmother was worried about possible problems.
3 Paragraph ⎯⎯ talks about a visit from her dad's cousin.
4 Paragraph ⎯⎯ says that they knew her dad wasn't happy.
5 Paragraph ⎯⎯ describes where Nina lived when she was a child.

b Read the text again and tick (✓) the best endings for the sentences.

1 Nina's mum went to live on the farm …
  a ☐ after Nina was born.
  b ✓ after she got married to Nina's dad.
  c ☐ when she was a child.

2 Nina's mum …
  a ☐ liked her husband's mother.
  b ☐ wanted a different house.
  c ☐ didn't like her husband's mother.

3 Nina knew that her dad …
  a ☐ was happy.
  b ☐ wanted a different job.
  c ☐ wasn't happy.

4 Nina's dad was unhappy when his cousin came because …
  a ☐ he didn't like his cousin.
  b ☐ he felt ill.
  c ☐ he didn't like being a farmer.

5 Nina's mum …
  a ☐ wanted to work on the farm.
  b ☐ wanted to become a teacher.
  c ☐ didn't want to work on the farm.

6 In the end, Nina's dad was happy because …
  a ☐ his cousin went away.
  b ☐ his children liked the farm.
  c ☐ he changed his job.

c Write about two people in your family who are older than you: your parents, your grandparents or two other people.

- Describe their lives when you were a small child.
- Did they live near you? In the same house? Far away from you?
- What were their jobs? Did they like them? Did they change jobs?

1 My family lived on a farm. It was my grandfather's farm. He and my dad worked together, and when Mum and Dad got married, Mum lived there, too. Soon they had three children – me and my brothers. It was a good place for children to grow up.

2 Mum's mother said it was a mistake to live with Dad's parents. She said that Mum and Dad needed a house of their own. But Mum liked it on the farm, and she and my grandmother became good friends.

3 So my grandparents weren't a problem. Mum was happy, and my brothers and I were happy. The problem was my dad. He said that everything was OK, but we all knew that something was wrong.

4 One day, my dad's cousin came to visit. He was an engineer, and he told us all about his interesting job. After he left, my dad looked really unhappy. That night, my mum asked him again what was wrong, and he told her. He hated the farm. He wanted to change his job, but he knew how important the farm was to his father. 'I don't know what to do,' he said.

5 Then my mum thought of a plan. 'I love the farm,' she said. 'I can be the farmer in the family! You can get a different job, and your parents can keep the farm.' So that's what they did. My mum became a farmer, my grandmother looked after us, and my dad went to college and became a teacher. After that, everyone was happy!

2 LISTENING

a ▶06.07 Listen to the conversation. Use the words in the box to make three sentences about the conversation.

> a lot   and uncle   brothers or sisters   have any
> love children   Maria doesn't   Maria has
> Maria's aunt   of cousins

b ▶06.07 Listen to the conversation again and complete the sentences.

1 Maria's cousins are all ____girls____.
2 Maria's cousin Tara has a _____ named Lexie.
3 Maria's cousin Mollie is Lexie's _____.
4 Maria's aunt and _____ always wanted to have a big family.
5 The cousins live in a big _____.
6 When she was young, Maria _____ a lot of time with her cousins.
7 Maria and her parents _____ near the cousins.
8 Maria's dad didn't _____ lots of children.

c Write about your brothers, sisters and cousins (or friends you have known for a long time). Remember to say:

- how many brothers, sisters and cousins you have
- how old they are
- how much time you spent with them when you were young and what you did together
- how much time you spend with them now
- what they are like and what they do now
- any other interesting things about them.

◉ Review and extension

1 GRAMMAR

Correct the sentences.

1 The weather were terrible when we was in New York.
The weather was terrible when we were in New York.
2 I payed for the meal with my credit card.
3 He eated all his vegetables.
4 They really enjoied the film.
5 Was you at work yesterday?
6 The ticket were very expensive. It costs £100!

2 VOCABULARY

Correct the sentences.

1 Hasan is angry because he losed his smartphone.
Hasan is angry because he lost his smartphone.
2 He telled me his name was Sergio.
3 They maked me a delicious chocolate cake.
4 Malika give me a ticket for the concert yesterday!
5 Last month, we winned a trip to Buenos Aires!
6 I red the paper and then I did the crossword.

3 WORDPOWER *go*

a Complete the conversation with the words in the box.

> for   home   out   shopping   to   by

MIA Hi, Bella. How was your weekend?
BELLA Oh, hello, Mia. It was really good, thanks. On Saturday night I went [1]____out____ to a restaurant with Luca.
MIA Really? Where?
BELLA We went [2]_____ the new Vietnamese restaurant in the city centre. It was really good.
MIA But isn't it far from your flat?
BELLA Yes, it is, so we went there [3]_____ bus. And we went [4]_____ by taxi.
MIA Lucky you! Do you want to go [5]_____ a walk?
BELLA No, I'm sorry, I can't. I need to go [6]_____. We haven't got anything for dinner.
MIA OK, never mind. See you soon!

b ▶06.08 Listen and check.

♻ REVIEW YOUR PROGRESS

Look again at Review your progress on p. 68 of the Student's Book. How well can you do these things now?
3 = very well   2 = well   1 = not so well

I CAN ...	
talk about my family and my family history	☐
talk about past activities and hobbies	☐
leave a voicemail message and ask for someone on the phone	☐
write a life story.	☐

7C EVERYDAY ENGLISH
Excuse me, please

1 USEFUL LANGUAGE
Saying *excuse me* and *I'm sorry*

a Complete the mini-conversations with the phrases in the box. (Sometimes there is more than one possible answer.)

It doesn't matter   Excuse me, please   That's OK
I'm so sorry (x2)   No problem   ~~Excuse me, but~~

A ¹ Excuse me, but I think that's my suitcase.
B Is it? ²_____. I took the wrong one.
A ³_____. They look the same.

A ⁴_____ I didn't come to your party.
B ⁵_____. Are you OK?
A I'm all right now, but I didn't feel well yesterday.

A ⁶_____. Can you explain that again, please?
B ⁷_____. German grammar is very hard.

b ▶️07.03 Listen and check.

c Match sentences 1–5 with sentences a-e.

1 [e] I'm very sorry I'm late.
2 [ ] I'm sorry I lost your keys.
3 [ ] I'm so sorry I broke your phone.
4 [ ] I'm sorry I hit your car.
5 [ ] I'm really sorry I didn't reply to your message.

a The road was very wet.
b It fell into the bath.
c I always lose things.
d Work was very busy today.
e I didn't hear my alarm.

d ▶️07.04 Listen and check.

2 PRONUNCIATION
Emphasising what we say

a ▶️07.05 Listen to the sentences and underline the stressed words.

1 He's very tired today.
2 I'm so sorry I'm late.
3 We're really busy at the moment.
4 It's very cold outside.
5 I'm really sorry I can't come.
6 We're so lost!

7D | SKILLS FOR WRITING
It really is hard to choose

1 READING

a Adriana Santos, a Brazilian student, studies at a university in London. Read her post on *Study Abroad Blog*, a blog about students' lives in other countries. Then tick (✓) the correct answer.

The blog talks about:
1 ☐ British transport, work and shopping
2 ☐ food, London, and studying English
3 ☐ Adriana's family, travelling in Mexico and her classes
4 ☐ Adriana's homestay family, her classes, and her future plans

b Read Adriana's post on *Study Abroad Blog* again. Are the sentences true (*T*) or false (*F*)?

1 Adriana doesn't like London.
2 Adriana likes living with the Henderson family.
3 Adriana has a long walk from the Hendersons' house to the university.
4 Adriana wants to study something new when she goes back to Brazil.
5 Adriana and Antonia want to go to a Shakespeare play in London.

2 WRITING SKILLS Linking ideas with *after*, *when* and *while*

a Match 1–6 with a–f to make sentences.

1 [e] I'd like to watch a film
2 ☐ I read my book
3 ☐ When we got to the hotel,
4 ☐ While I'm in Thailand,
5 ☐ I'd like to go to Spain on holiday
6 ☐ She said goodbye to her homestay family

a when they got to the airport.
b after I graduate from university.
c I'd like to visit Koh Samui.
d while I was on the beach.
e after I finish my homework.
f we had a quick snack and then went to bed.

3 WRITING

a Imagine you live and study in another country. Write a post on *Study Abroad Blog*. Try to use linking words (*after*, *when*, *while*). Think about:
- the places in the city
- where you live and who you live with
- your studies
- people you know.

Study Abroad Blog

The city: London's a great city, but it's so big. There are lots of interesting places to visit and there are many restaurants and theatres, so I'm never bored!

Where I live: I have a room with a British family here. They're very nice. Mr Henderson's a chef and Mrs Henderson's a nurse. They've got two children, Zoe and Mark. Zoe loves playing the piano and Mark likes playing computer games. Their house is near the Underground station, so it only takes about 25 minutes to get to university.

What I do here: My course is very interesting. My favourite class is North American History. After we finish, the teacher often goes to a café with us to talk more about our studies. It's great fun! I want to study more history when I go back to Brazil next year.

Who I know: I have a lot of friends on my course – they're all so friendly. My best friend's Antonia. She's from Guadalajara in Mexico. She's 22 and she loves going to the theatre with me. We'd like to see a Shakespeare play while we're in London, but the tickets are really expensive.

Study Abroad Blog

The city:
_____
_____
_____
_____

Where I live:
_____
_____
_____
_____

What I do here:
_____
_____
_____
_____

Who I know:
_____
_____
_____

43

1 READING

a Read the text. Are the sentences true (*T*) or false (*F*)?

1 Tom loved going to the mountains.
2 He didn't go to the mountains very often.
3 This time, he didn't know how to get home.

b Complete the sentences about the text with the words in the box.

| ~~cost~~ | find | heard | slept | thought | used | walked | went |

1 Tom's flat _____cost_____ a lot of money.
2 At the weekend, he _____ to the mountains.
3 When he walked in the mountains, he _____ in a tent.
4 He _____ a lot about his job in the city.
5 On the second day, he tried to _____ a road.
6 For three days, he _____ in a straight line.
7 He knew the helicopter was there because he _____ it.
8 He _____ his shirt to help the pilot see him.

c Write a short story about a trip with a problem. Think about these questions:

• Why was the person on the trip?
• What was the problem?
• What happened in the end?

LOST IN THE MOUNTAINS!

1 Tom Roberts hated living in the city. He thought it was noisy and crowded, and his flat was so expensive, he spent most of his money on it.

2 All week at work he thought about the weekends, when he could get away to the countryside. On Fridays, he packed his tent and some food and water, and caught a bus to the mountains. That was where he felt really happy. He didn't mind camping, even in winter – he just took a very warm sleeping bag!

3 One weekend, he went to the mountains as usual. He followed a path into a forest. He enjoyed the silence and the clean, fresh air. He thought about his job and the city where he lived. He decided that he wanted a new job, away from the city. But what job could he do in the countryside? He thought about all of this, and he didn't think about where he was going.

4 Then he stopped. He felt cold. It was dark. And he had no idea where he was.

5 He tried to walk in a straight line. He was sure he must come to a road soon! Three days later, he was still walking. By now, he was hungry, dirty and afraid. He started to think that he could never get out of the mountains. Then he heard a strange noise. The noise got louder and louder until at last he saw a helicopter in the air above him.

6 Tom knew this was his last chance. He took off his red shirt, climbed onto a large rock and waved it. When the helicopter flew closer, he knew he was safe at last.

2 LISTENING

a ▶ 07.06 Listen to the conversation. <u>Underline</u> the correct words to complete the sentences.

1 Lara <u>has</u> / *doesn't have* a lot of money.
2 Rick *has* / *doesn't have* a lot of money.
3 Lara probably *likes* / *doesn't like* holidays like Rick's holiday.

b ▶ 07.06 Listen to the conversation again. Tick (✓) the correct words to complete the sentences.

1 Lara travelled to France by …
  a ☐ ship.
  b ✓ aeroplane.
  c ☐ train.
2 Rick travelled to France by …
  a ☐ ferry.
  b ☐ bike.
  c ☐ train.
3 While he was in France, Rick travelled around by …
  a ☐ train.
  b ☐ ferry.
  c ☐ bike.
4 Rick loves riding his bike in …
  a ☐ the city.
  b ☐ towns.
  c ☐ the countryside.
5 Lara stayed …
  a ☐ in people's homes.
  b ☐ in a hotel.
  c ☐ with friends.
6 Rick stayed …
  a ☐ in people's homes.
  b ☐ in a hotel.
  c ☐ with friends.
7 Lara ate her meals …
  a ☐ in restaurants.
  b ☐ on the beach.
  c ☐ in cafés.
8 At the end of her holiday, Lara …
  a ☐ took her plane.
  b ☐ caught her plane.
  c ☐ missed her plane.

c Write a conversation between two people about holidays. One has a lot of money, and one doesn't.

• Describe where each person went and the things they did.
• What difference did it make to have a lot of money or not much money?

 Review and extension

1 GRAMMAR

Correct the sentences.

1 Did you watched the football match last night?
  Did you watch the football match last night?
2 We didn't stayed in expensive hotels.
3 I didn't liked the food in that restaurant.
4 **A** Did they catch the last bus?
  B Yes, they do.
5 He didn't came to the cinema with us because he was tired.
6 Did you bought your sunglasses in the supermarket?
7 Nico didn't wanted to wait for the bus.
8 **A** Did he go to his grandparents' house on Sunday?
  B No, he don't.

2 VOCABULARY

Correct the sentences.

1 Sho lost his plane and waited five hours for the next one.
  Sho missed his plane and waited five hours for the next one.
2 We hit the train every day at 8 o'clock.
3 Get up at the next stop for the museum.
4 You don't check planes to go to Sydney. It's a direct flight.
5 I didn't put on the bus because it was full.
6 Maryam gives the tram to go to the city centre.

3 WORDPOWER *get*

Change one verb in each sentence to the correct form of the verb *get*.

1 Are you thirsty? Have a glass of water.
  Are you thirsty? Get a glass of water.
2 He becomes angry when we're late for class.
3 We arrived here early today.
4 I received a letter from an old friend last week.
5 I bought a new bag this morning.

↻ REVIEW YOUR PROGRESS

Look again at Review your progress on p. 78 of the Student's Book. How well can you do these things now?
3 = very well   2 = well   1 = not so well

I CAN …	
talk about past trips	☐
talk about what I like and dislike about transport	☐
say *excuse me* and *I'm sorry*	☐
write an email about myself.	☐

8A | THEY CAN DO THINGS MOST PEOPLE CAN'T

1 GRAMMAR
can / can't; *could / couldn't* for ability

a Look at the questionnaire about Altan and complete the sentences with *can* or *can't*.

1 Altan __can__ ski quite well, but he __can't__ skate at all.
2 **NAM** _____ you ride a horse, Altan?
  ALTAN No, I _____, but I _____ ride a bike really well!
3 Altan _____ sing very well. He _____ play the piano quite well, but he _____ play the guitar at all.
4 **NAM** _____ you do yoga?
  ALTAN Yes, I _____ do yoga really well.
5 He _____ do karate quite well, but he _____ do judo at all.

Altan's abilities questionnaire				
	Yes, really well	Yes, quite well	No, not very well	No, not at all
ski?	◯	✓	◯	◯
skate?	◯	◯	◯	✓
ride a horse?	◯	◯	◯	✓
ride a bike?	✓	◯	◯	◯
sing?	◯	◯	✓	◯
play the piano?	◯	✓	◯	◯
play the guitar?	◯	◯	◯	✓
do yoga?	✓	◯	◯	◯
do judo?	◯	◯	◯	✓
do karate?	◯	✓	◯	◯

b Underline the correct words to complete the sentences.

1 My mother *can / couldn't / can't* swim when she was a child, but now she *can / could / couldn't* swim five kilometres.
2 **A** *Can / Can't / Could* you play tennis when you were five?
  B No, I *can't / couldn't / could*.
3 **A** *Can / Can't / Couldn't* you speak Spanish?
  B No, not now. I *can / can't / could* speak it when I lived in Mexico, but not any more.
4 When I started cycling, I *can't / couldn't / can* ride very far, but now I *could / can / can't* ride ten kilometres without stopping.
5 He *could / can't / can* dance all night when he was a young man, but not these days.
6 I usually work at weekends, so I *could / can / can't* play golf very often.

2 VOCABULARY Sport and exercise

a Complete the sentences.

1 He went ___running___ every day after work because he wanted to get fit for the London Marathon.
2 At weekends, my father _____ his _____ in the mountains. He often cycles more than 100 km.
3 John loves going _____. He likes spending the day by the river. When he catches something, he likes to cook it for dinner.
4 I went to Switzerland last winter, and I went _____ in the mountains every day.
5 Sometimes I do _____ in the evening. It helps me to relax before I go to bed.
6 Alicia loves going _____ at the sports centre pool. The water is always nice and warm.
7 I like playing _____ on the beach. You only need four people, a ball and a net.
8 In Argentina, I learned to _____ the tango.
9 In Quebec, it's so cold in the winter that you can _____ on the river.
10 Last summer, we went _____ on a big boat on the Mediterranean Sea for a week. I'd love to do it again.

3 PRONUNCIATION
can, can't, could and *couldn't*

▶ 08.01 Listen to *can* and *can't* in the sentences and tick (✓) the correct sound.

	Sound 1 /æ/ (e.g. *cat*)	Sound 2 /ɑː/ (e.g. *car*)
a Can you speak French?	✓	
b Yes, I can.		
c I can't ski very well.		
d Can he play the piano?		
e No, he can't.		
f We can take the train to Manchester.		
g She can't play tennis very well.		
h He can't run that fast.		

8B | HOW EASY IS IT TO GET FIT?

1 GRAMMAR *have to / don't have to*

a <u>Underline</u> the correct words to complete the sentences.

1 **A** *You have to / Do you have to / Have you to* be really fit to run a half marathon?
   B Yes, *you have / you have to / you do*. You *have to / have / has to* train hard for months.

2 They learned Spanish when they lived in Spain, so they *haven't to / don't have to / doesn't have to* study hard for the Spanish exam.

3 If you want to become a really good athlete, you *have to / has to / haven't to* train every day.

4 **A** *Had you to / You had to / Did you have to* take a taxi to the airport?
   B Yes, *we did / we had to / we had*.

5 **A** *Have you to / Do you have to / You have to* go to the gym every day if you want to get fit?
   B No, *you haven't / you have not / you don't*, but you *has to / have to / have* go three times a week.

b Complete each sentence with the correct form of *have to*.

1 **A** _____Do_____ you ___have to___ bring your own skis?
   B No, you _____. You can hire them for the day.

2 You _____ pay to use the gym for a day. It's free if you want to try it.

3 Sometimes she can work from home, so she _____ go to the office every day.

4 In some countries, children _____ go to school in the evenings. I think it's better to go in the mornings.

5 **A** _____ I _____ become a member to use the swimming pool?
   B Yes, you _____.

6 **A** What time _____ she _____ catch the bus to school in the morning?
   B She _____ get the bus at 7:30 because she lives far from her school.

2 VOCABULARY Parts of the body

a Match the parts of the body in the picture with the words in the box.

arm	hand	leg	foot	stomach	head	neck	knee

1 _____
2 _____
3 _____
4 _____
5 _____
6 _____
7 _____
8 _____

b Complete the crossword puzzle.

→ Across

4 He can't hold a pen or pencil because he broke two of his ___fingers___ in the accident.

6 I don't like dancing with you. You always step on my _____.

7 This bed is really uncomfortable. It gives me a bad _____.

↓ Down

1 I think these shoes are too small for me. They hurt my _____.

2 You've got a thumb and four fingers on each _____.

3 You have to have strong _____ to run a marathon.

4 He can't walk very far at the moment because his _____ hurts.

5 When I sleep on a plane, my head falls to the side, and then my _____ hurts.

8 Lucas broke his _____ when he went skiing last weekend.

8C EVERYDAY ENGLISH
I feel a bit tired

1 USEFUL LANGUAGE
Talking about health and how you feel

a Match questions 1–5 with answers a–e.

1 [c] What's the matter?
2 [ ] How do you feel?
3 [ ] Are you all right?
4 [ ] Does your knee hurt?
5 [ ] Have you got a temperature?

a Yes, it does. It hurts when I walk.
b No, I haven't. I just feel a bit tired.
c Nothing. I've just got a bit of a stomach ache.
d Yes, I'm fine now, thanks.
e Well, actually, I feel really awful.

b ▶08.02 Listen and check.

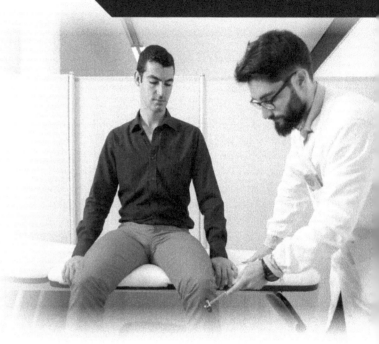

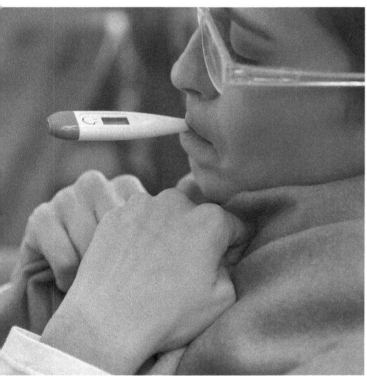

c Put the conversation in the correct order.

[ ] **TONY** You don't look very well.
[ ] **TONY** Do you feel sick?
[ ] **JUDY** Well, actually, I don't feel very well.
[ ] **JUDY** I think I've got a temperature.
[ ] **JUDY** OK, thanks.
[1] **TONY** Hi, Judy. Good to see you. How are you?
[ ] **TONY** You poor thing! Come and sit down. I'll get you a glass of water.
[ ] **JUDY** Er, I'm not sure.
[ ] **JUDY** Yes, a bit, and I've got an awful headache.
[ ] **TONY** Hey, Judy. Are you all right?

d ▶08.03 Listen and check.

2 PRONUNCIATION Joining words

a ▶08.04 Listen to the sentences. Tick (✓) the two words that are joined together.

1 That man over there doesn't dance very well.
   a [ ] very well   b [✓] doesn't dance
2 My uncle has got two big dogs.
   a [ ] uncle has   b [ ] got two
3 Thank you very much, madam. Have a good day.
   a [ ] very much   b [ ] good day
4 We've got a really big garden at our house.
   a [ ] big garden   b [ ] our house
5 There's a small lake in the middle of the park.
   a [ ] small lake   b [ ] the park

8D | SKILLS FOR WRITING
However, I improved quickly

1 READING

a Every month, *Pastimes* magazine interviews a reader about their hobby. Read Nick Delgado's interview and tick (✓) the best answer.

Nick likes taking photos …
1. ☐ when he goes on holiday with friends.
2. ☐ of different people and places.
3. ☐ when there is a competition he can enter.

b Read the interview again. Are the sentences true (*T*) or false (*F*)?

1. ☐ Nick became interested in photography when he saw his friend's photos of Machu Picchu.
2. ☐ Nick's first camera wasn't very expensive.
3. ☐ Nick prefers to print his photos to show people.
4. ☐ Nick's grandfather won a prize in the photography competition.
5. ☐ Nick wants to become a professional photographer.

Nick, tell us why you started your hobby.

Two years ago, a friend showed me some photos from his holiday in Peru. His photos of Machu Picchu were really amazing, so I decided to start taking photos, too.

So, what did you do next?

I bought a cheap camera and carried it everywhere with me. I took photos of my family, my friends and the countryside near my town.
I joined a photography club and slowly improved. However, I only had an old laptop, and I couldn't see the photos very well or show them to friends easily. I decided to buy a computer with a really big screen. Now everyone can see the photos clearly, and I can make changes to the colours quickly and easily.

Last month, I entered a photography competition, and a photo of my grandfather won first prize. I was so happy! I won £500, so I bought a fantastic new camera.

What would you like to do with your hobby in the future?

I'd really like to be a professional photographer. However, there aren't a lot of jobs for photographers, so at the moment it's only a hobby.

2 WRITING SKILLS
Adverbs of manner

a Complete the sentences with adverbs formed from the adjectives in brackets.

1. The Tour de France riders cycled __slowly__ (slow) up the mountain and then went down the other side really __fast__ (fast).
2. My football team lost the match 8–0 because we played very _____ (bad).
3. If you listen _____ (careful), you can hear the sound of the sea in the distance.
4. When you travel, you can make new friends _____ (easy).
5. My phone doesn't work very _____ (good) here, so please speak _____ (clear).
6. You can fly to Bangkok very _____ (cheap) these days.

3 WRITING

a Think about the hobby/sport of a person in your family or a famous person you like. Write answers to the questions. Remember to use adverbs.

When and why did he/she start the hobby/sport?
_____
_____
_____
_____
_____

What did he/she do (e.g., clubs, competitions)?
_____
_____
_____
_____
_____

What would he/she like to do with the hobby/sport in the future?
_____
_____
_____
_____
_____

1 READING

a Read the magazine article. Tick (✓) the best description of what it says.

1 ☐ Triathlons are very difficult, and you can only do them if you are very fit.

2 ☐ There are triathlons at different levels, so you can find one that is right for you. You can prepare for a triathlon at any level.

3 ☐ It is easy to swim, bike or run, but it is difficult to do all three with no rest in between. It is best not to try to do these things together.

b Read the magazine article again and complete the sentences.

1 In the first part of the triathlon you have to ___swim___, often in a lake or the sea.

2 When you swim in the sea, you can't usually put your _____ down.

3 When you practise swimming, lift your _____ a long way out of the water.

4 In the second part of the triathlon, you have to _____ a bike.

5 It's dangerous to get too _____ to the other bikes.

6 When you start to run, you usually feel _____.

c Write an email to a friend who never does any sport. Give him or her some ideas about one or two sports to try and some advice about how to prepare. Include at least one sentence with *have to* and one with *don't have to*.

HOW TO PREPARE FOR A
TRIATHLON

So, you can swim, you can ride a bike and you go running twice a week. But all three things together ... Are you crazy?

Many people like the idea of a triathlon, but they're worried that it's too difficult for them. If that's you, remember, you don't have to start with the Olympics. There are a lot of triathlons for beginners.

So read our advice and start preparing for your first triathlon. *You can do it!*

🏊 SWIMMING

For many people, it's the first part, swimming, that they're most worried about. It's often in a lake or the sea, so, even if you get tired, you can't put your feet down for a rest. Also, you have to lift your arms up high because the water moves up and down. It's a good idea to practise this, even when you're in the swimming pool.

🚴 CYCLING

This is the second part of the triathlon. Riding a bike with a lot of other people can be strange at first, so practise with friends. Remember that, in the race, you have to stay away from the other bikes because it's dangerous to get too close.

🏃 RUNNING

The running part is often very hard because you have to do it when you're already tired. When you get off the bike, you may think you can't even stand up! So make sure you practise riding your bike and then running at least once a week.

GOOD LUCK!

2 LISTENING

a ▶ 08.05 Listen to the conversation. Are the sentences true (*T*) or false (*F*)?

1 Rosa can play badminton today.
2 Rosa and Emilia talk about doing exercises for Rosa's back.
3 Rosa and Emilia don't want to try yoga.

b ▶ 08.05 Listen to the conversation again. Who are the sentences about, Rosa (R) or Emilia (E)?

1 [R] Her back hurts.
2 [ ] Her dad has problems with his back.
3 [ ] Her mum does yoga.
4 [ ] She can't touch her toes.
5 [ ] She fell over when she was ice skating.
6 [ ] She has a lecture at two.
7 [ ] She has to be careful about her back.
8 [ ] She is learning to play the piano.
9 [ ] She needs to find another friend to play badminton.
10 [ ] She says there are yoga classes online.
11 [ ] She thinks yoga is difficult.

c ▶ 08.05 Listen again. Underline the correct words to complete the sentences.

1 Rosa fell and hurt her *leg* / *back* / *hand*.
2 She was ice skating with her *friend* / *mum* / *sister*.
3 When she fell, it *didn't hurt much* / *hurt a lot* / *hurt a bit*.
4 Rosa's *sister* / *dad* / *mum* has a bad back, too.
5 Emilia's mum says that *yoga* / *badminton* / *skating* is good for your back.
6 Rosa and Emilia decide to *go to a yoga class* / *play badminton* / *go ice skating*.

d Write about the sports you do. Think about these questions:

- Which sports do you do?
- What do you have to do?
- Why do you like the sports?

If you don't do any sports, write about why not. Think about these questions:

- Why don't you do any sports?
- Is there a reason you can't do them?
- Which sports would you like to try and why?

 Review and extension

1 GRAMMAR

Correct the sentences.

1 My brother can skiing very well.
   My *brother can ski very well.*
2 When I was 15, I could ran 100 metres in 12 seconds.
3 I'm sorry I couldn't coming to your party.
4 My grandfather can't to see very well without his glasses.
5 Can you dancing the tango?
6 He couldn't to play football after he broke his leg.
7 Helen could drove when she was 17.
8 Could you to ride a bike when you were five?

2 VOCABULARY

Correct the sentences.

1 When they were at the beach, they played football and voleyball.
   When they were at the beach, they played football and volleyball.
2 We went runing after work yesterday.
3 I love skying in the winter.
4 We don't play tenis in the rain.
5 Snowbording is a very popular sport in Chile.
6 I don't like going fisching. It's so boring!
7 I couldn't danse very well before I took lessons.
8 He goes swiming every day before work.

3 WORDPOWER *tell / say*

Complete the sentences with the words in the box.

told   say   tells   ~~said~~   tell   said

1 Alba _____said_____ sorry for being late.
2 I _____ my wife I was at the airport.
3 Please _____ sorry to your sister that I forgot her birthday.
4 My uncle always _____ us about what he did in the war.
5 We _____ goodbye at the airport last night.
6 Can you _____ me how to get to the train station, please?

🔄 REVIEW YOUR PROGRESS

Look again at Review your progress on p. 88 of the Student's Book. How well can you do these things now?
3 = very well   2 = well   1 = not so well

I CAN ...	
talk about past and present abilities	[ ]
talk about sport and exercise	[ ]
talk about the body and getting fit	[ ]
talk about health and how I feel	[ ]
write an article.	[ ]

9A | WE AREN'T BUYING ANYTHING

1 VOCABULARY Shopping

a Write the names of the places in a shopping centre under the pictures.

1 _department store_

2 _____

3 _____

4 _____

5 _____

6 _____

2 GRAMMAR Present continuous

a <u>Underline</u> the correct words to complete the sentences.

1 **A** What *do you doing* / <u>*are you doing*</u> / *you are doing* here?
  B I *'m waiting* / *'s waiting* / *waiting* for my brother.
2 **A** Where *Michael is going* / *Michael going* / *'s Michael going*?
  B *He looking* / *He's looking* / *Is he looking* for his brother.
3 **A** *Are you having* / *You're having* / *You having* your dinner now?
  B Yes, *we do* / *we're having* / *we are*. We *having* / *are have* / *'re having* spaghetti bolognese.
4 **A** What *you're buying* / *are you buying* / *you buying*?
  B I *'m not buying* / *not buying* / *'m not buy* anything. I *just looking* / *just are looking* / *'m just looking*.
5 **A** It *'s raining not* / *not raining* / *isn't raining* at the moment.
  B In fact, the sun *shining* / *are shining* / *'s shining* now.

b ▶09.01 Listen and check.

c Complete the sentences with the present continuous form of the verbs in brackets. Use contractions where possible.

1 **A** What __'s Silvia doing__? (Silvia, do)
  B She _____ (get) ready to go out.
2 **A** Who _____ (you, wait) for?
  B I _____ (wait) for my friend.
3 **A** _____ (you and Fatima, have) a good time in Cyprus?
  B No, _____ (not). We _____ (stay) at a horrible hotel.
4 **A** What _____ (you, read) at the moment?
  B I _____ (read) the new novel by the author of the Harry Potter books.
5 Julian _____ (buy) some new jeans.
6 How funny! Rodrigo and Martin _____ (wear) the same shirt!

3 PRONUNCIATION Word stress in compound nouns

a ▶09.02 Listen and decide which word is stressed. Tick (✓) the stressed word.

1 This is one of the biggest shopping centres in the world.
  a ✓ shopping   b ☐ centres
2 There are over two hundred and fifty clothes shops.
  a ☐ clothes   b ☐ shops
3 There are about twenty-three bookshops.
  a ☐ book   b ☐ shops
4 If you can't find a shop, you can ask someone at the information desk for help.
  a ☐ information   b ☐ desk
5 It can be hard to find a space in the car park.
  a ☐ car   b ☐ park
6 I waited for over an hour at the bus stop.
  a ☐ bus   b ☐ stop

9B EVERYONE'S DANCING IN THE STREETS

1 GRAMMAR Present simple or present continuous

a <u>Underline</u> the correct words to complete the conversation.

EMMA Hi, Joe. What ¹*do you buy* / <u>*are you buying*</u>?

JOE Hello, Emma. ²*I'm buying* / *I buy* some new trousers.

EMMA But ³*you're usually wearing* / *you usually wear* jeans and trainers.

JOE Yes, ⁴*I'm knowing* / *I know*. ⁵*I'm trying* / *I try* to dress smartly in my new job.

EMMA Well, ⁶*I'm liking* / *I like* them.

JOE Good, and, look, ⁷*I wear* / *I'm wearing* some new shoes that I bought yesterday.

EMMA Wow, ⁸*they're looking* / *they look* great!

JOE Thanks. ⁹*Are you wearing* / *Do you wear* a new dress?

EMMA Yes, ¹⁰*I do* / *I am*. What ¹¹*are you thinking* / *do you think*?

JOE It's really nice. Hey, ¹²*do you want* / *are you wanting* to go for a coffee?

EMMA Sorry, I can't. ¹³*I wait* / *I'm waiting* for my boyfriend. ¹⁴*He's parking* / *He parks* the car.

JOE OK, never mind. Bye!

b ▶09.03 Listen and check.

c Complete the sentences. Use the present simple or present continuous forms of the verbs in the box.

---
walk   spend   cost   drink   ~~wear~~
watch   wait   go   rain   ~~like~~
---

1 Mako never ___wears___ dresses to work. She ___likes___ wearing trousers.
2 He can't talk to you at the moment. He _____ a football match on TV.
3 I _____ for you in front of the train station. Don't be late!
4 We normally _____ orange juice with breakfast and water with lunch.
5 It _____ more than £1,000 to buy a ticket for the World Cup!
6 It _____ hard now, so we can't go for a walk by the river.
7 We often _____ our holidays in the mountains.
8 Yes, we usually _____ home by bus, but we _____ home now.

2 VOCABULARY Clothes

a Complete the crossword puzzle.

→ Across
2 I usually wear blue _____. But I've got other kinds of trousers, too.
4 You wear _____ to cover your feet. They are very soft.
7 My grandma gave me this beautiful _____. Unfortunately, it's too small for my finger.
8 Look at those dark clouds! Why don't you take your _____ with you?
11 It's more comfortable to wear _____ on a hot day than trousers.

↓ Down
1 That wedding ___dress___ costs £10,000. It's too expensive!
3 At my sister's school, the boys have to wear trousers, and the girls have to wear a _____.
5 David needs a new white _____ and a tie to wear for his job interview on Monday.
6 Your hands look so cold! Where are your _____?
9 If you want to know the time, look at your _____.
10 In the snow, you should wear _____ on your feet. They keep your feet warm and dry.

3 PRONUNCIATION Sound and spelling: *o*

a ▶09.04 Listen to the words with *o*. Complete the table with the words in the box.

~~vote~~   some   soup   dollar   rock   pool   other   toe
boat   brother   cool   on   cough   do   love   hope

/ɒ/ (e.g., *sock*)	/uː/ (e.g., *boot*)	/ʌ/ (e.g., *glove*)	/əʊ/ (e.g., *coat*)
			vote

9C EVERYDAY ENGLISH
It looks really good on you

1 USEFUL LANGUAGE
Choosing and paying for clothes

a Match questions 1–6 with answers a–f.

1. ☐ *d* Can I help you?
2. ☐ Can I try them on?
3. ☐ What size are you?
4. ☐ What colour would you like?
5. ☐ What do you think?
6. ☐ How much are these jeans, please?

a Blue or green, please.
b 32, I think.
c They're £49.99.
d Yes, I'm looking for a red dress and some smart shoes.
e It looks really good on you.
f Certainly. The fitting rooms are over there.

b ▶ 09.05 Listen and check.

c Put the words in the correct order to make sentences.

1. looking / some / for / jeans / I'm .
   I'm looking for some jeans.
2. a / I'm / 10 / size .
   _____
3. would / colour / like / what / you ?
   _____
4. size / think / I / are / these / your .
   _____
5. over / fitting / rooms / the / there / just / are .
   _____
6. you / on / they / great / look .
   _____
7. them / take / I'll .
   _____
8. I / card / by / credit / pay / can ?
   _____

2 PRONUNCIATION Joining words

a ▶ 09.06 Listen to the sentences. Tick (✓) the two words that are joined together.

1. I'm a size 10.
   a ✓ I'm a
   b ☐ size 10
2. It looks good on you.
   a ☐ good on
   b ☐ on you
3. How much is it?
   a ☐ How much
   b ☐ much is
4. The jeans are over there.
   a ☐ The jeans
   b ☐ jeans are

54

9D SKILLS FOR WRITING
Thank you for the nice present

1 READING

a Read the four thank-you emails. Which email is from … ?

  a ☐ someone who was ill recently
  b ☐ someone who had a problem with her car
  c ☐ a family member
  d ☐ 1 someone who left her company

1

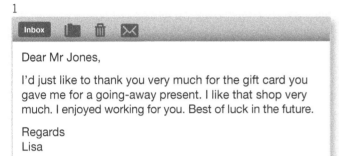

> **Inbox** 📁 🗑 ✉
>
> Dear Mr Jones,
>
> I'd just like to thank you very much for the gift card you gave me for a going-away present. I like that shop very much. I enjoyed working for you. Best of luck in the future.
>
> Regards
> Lisa

2

> ◀ Inbox
>
> Hello Grandma,
>
> Thanks very much for the shirt you gave me for my birthday. It's a lovely present! Blue's my favourite colour, and my friends say it looks really good on me.
>
> Love
> Tina

3

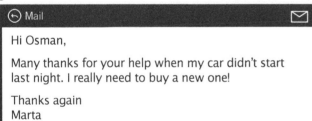

> ↩ Mail ✉
>
> Hi Osman,
>
> Many thanks for your help when my car didn't start last night. I really need to buy a new one!
>
> Thanks again
> Marta

4

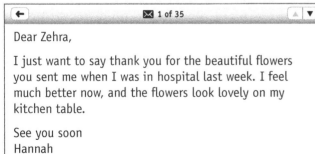

> ← ✉ 1 of 35 ▲ ▼
>
> Dear Zehra,
>
> I just want to say thank you for the beautiful flowers you sent me when I was in hospital last week. I feel much better now, and the flowers look lovely on my kitchen table.
>
> See you soon
> Hannah

b Read the emails again. Are the sentences true (*T*) or false (*F*)?

1 Lisa bought Mr Jones a gift card when she left her job.
2 Tina didn't like her birthday present from her grandmother.
3 Marta helped Osman start his car yesterday.
4 Hannah isn't in hospital this week.

2 WRITING SKILLS Writing formal and informal emails

a Add one word to each sentence to make it correct.

1 I just wanted to thank you the lovely present you gave me.
  <u>I just wanted to thank you for the lovely present you gave me.</u>

2 Thanks much for the book you sent me for my birthday.
  _____

3 I just wanted thank you for the flowers.
  _____

4 Thank for the chocolates. They were delicious!
  _____

5 I just like to say thank you for inviting me to your party on Saturday.
  _____

3 WRITING

a Write two thank-you emails. Use the information in the boxes and the emails in 1a to help you.

Email 1

To: Sonia

Relationship: your friend

Reason for writing: to thank her for her help when you moved to a new flat

Extra information: the new flat = lovely, invite her for dinner soon?

From: Irena

Email 2

To: Ana

Relationship: your mum's neighbour

Reason for writing: to thank her for looking after your cat (Bob) when you were on holiday

Extra information: lovely holiday, cup of coffee at your house?

From: Miguel

1 READING

a Read the two emails. Complete the sentences.

1 Owen sent Rafael an ___invitation___ to visit him.
2 Rafael wants to know about the _____ where Owen lives.
3 Owen describes the shops and cafés in his _____.
4 Owen tells Rafael about the _____ in Wales in summer.
5 Owen tells Rafael what _____ he needs to bring.

b Complete the sentences with the words in the box. There are some extra words.

countryside difficult easy food ~~invited~~
shops sister Canada Wales weather

1 Owen ___invited___ Rafael to visit him.
2 Rafael and his family are skiing in _____.
3 Rafael's _____ isn't always nice to him.
4 There aren't many _____ in the town where Owen lives.
5 It is _____ to get to a city where there are lots of things to do.
6 The _____ in the summer isn't always good.

c A friend from another country is coming to visit you. Write an email describing the place where you live and the clothes your friend needs to bring.

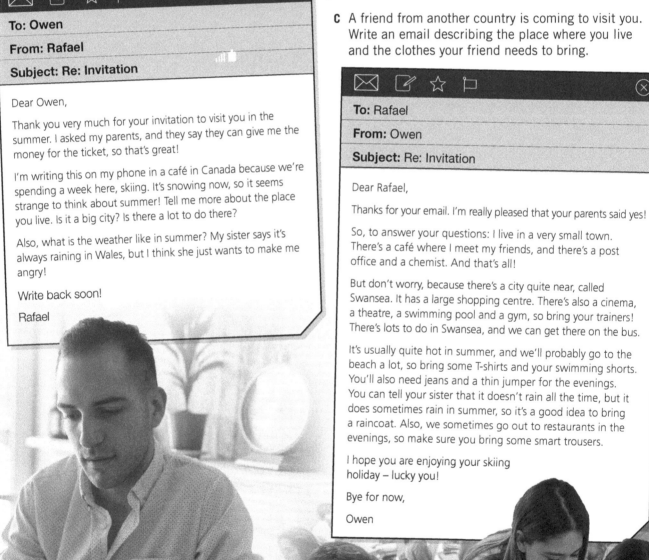

To: Owen

From: Rafael

Subject: Re: Invitation

Dear Owen,

Thank you very much for your invitation to visit you in the summer. I asked my parents, and they say they can give me the money for the ticket, so that's great!

I'm writing this on my phone in a café in Canada because we're spending a week here, skiing. It's snowing now, so it seems strange to think about summer! Tell me more about the place you live. Is it a big city? Is there a lot to do there?

Also, what is the weather like in summer? My sister says it's always raining in Wales, but I think she just wants to make me angry!

Write back soon!

Rafael

To: Rafael

From: Owen

Subject: Re: Invitation

Dear Rafael,

Thanks for your email. I'm really pleased that your parents said yes!

So, to answer your questions: I live in a very small town. There's a café where I meet my friends, and there's a post office and a chemist. And that's all!

But don't worry, because there's a city quite near, called Swansea. It has a large shopping centre. There's also a cinema, a theatre, a swimming pool and a gym, so bring your trainers! There's lots to do in Swansea, and we can get there on the bus.

It's usually quite hot in summer, and we'll probably go to the beach a lot, so bring some T-shirts and your swimming shorts. You'll also need jeans and a thin jumper for the evenings. You can tell your sister that it doesn't rain all the time, but it does sometimes rain in summer, so it's a good idea to bring a raincoat. Also, we sometimes go out to restaurants in the evenings, so make sure you bring some smart trousers.

I hope you are enjoying your skiing holiday – lucky you!

Bye for now,

Owen

2 LISTENING

a ▶ 09.07 Listen to the conversations. Are the sentences true (*T*) or false (*F*)?

1 The family is having a birthday party for Grandma.
2 The children like what their dad is wearing.
3 Their grandmother will like what their dad is wearing.
4 Their dad has a good reason for wearing the jumper.

b ▶ 09.07 Listen to the conversations again and tick (✓) the correct answers.

1 What is on Dad's jumper?
  a ☐ a sheep
  b ✓ an elephant
  c ☐ eleven animals
2 What is the special day?
  a ☐ Grandma's birthday
  b ☐ Mum's birthday
  c ☐ Dad's birthday
3 What do Mum and Dad get from the kitchen?
  a ☐ glasses
  b ☐ a different jumper
  c ☐ sandwiches
4 Why does Grandma arrive early?
  a ☐ to see Dad's jumper
  b ☐ to eat some food
  c ☐ to help make the food
5 What food is Mum making when Grandma arrives?
  a ☐ pizza
  b ☐ cakes
  c ☐ sandwiches
6 Why does Dad say he needs to take off his jumper?
  a ☐ because he's too hot
  b ☐ because his children don't like it
  c ☐ because it's dirty
7 What is Dad wearing under the jumper?
  a ☐ an old shirt
  b ☐ a T-shirt
  c ☐ his best shirt
8 Why did Dad wear the jumper?
  a ☐ to please his mum
  b ☐ to please his wife
  c ☐ to make his children angry

c Think of somewhere special you went, for example a party or for a meal in an expensive restaurant. Write about the clothes that you and other people wore.

◉ Review and extension

1 GRAMMAR

Correct the sentences. (Sometimes there is more than one possible answer.)

1 Hi, Sofia! I really enjoy my holiday in Queensland.
  Hi, Sofia! I'm really enjoying my holiday in Queensland.
2 My friend Mario is speaking English very well.
3 Sorry, it's time to go because my train comes.
4 She's wait for us outside the cinema.
5 Daiki's in that shop over there. He buys a newspaper.
6 I'm usually going to the cinema at the weekend.
7 Mustafa's at the library. He's studies for his exams.
8 Are you liking Italian food?

2 VOCABULARY

Correct the sentences.

1 Jane is looking for a dress in that new clothes' shop.
  Jane is looking for a dress in that new clothes shop.
2 The quemist opposite the café is open all night.
3 He's waiting for us at the main entrace.
4 The booksshop closes at 5:30.
5 Excuse me. What's the prize of these jeans?
6 Here are your T-shirts. The reciept is in the bag.
7 I like your new skarf. It's very nice.
8 My boyfriend bought me these earings for my birthday.

3 WORDPOWER *time*

Complete the sentences with the words in the box.

| took   save   spend   ~~waste~~   spare   find   nice |

1 Don't ___waste___ time trying to find the street on your satnav. Just ask that woman over there.
2 It _____ him a long time to learn Chinese.
3 She loves going for long walks in her _____ time.
4 We can _____ time if we walk this way.
5 I hope you had a _____ time in Brazil.
6 It's really important to _____ time with your children when they are little.
7 I can never _____ time to read books.

◔ REVIEW YOUR PROGRESS

Look again at Review your progress on p. 98 of the Student's Book. How well can you do these things now?
3 = very well   2 = well   1 = not so well

I CAN ...	
say where I am and what I'm doing	☐
talk about the clothes I wear at different times	☐
shop for clothes	☐
write a thank-you email.	☐

10A | THEY'RE MORE COMFORTABLE THAN EARBUDS

1 GRAMMAR Comparative adjectives

a Underline the correct words to complete the sentences.

1 My new laptop is *more light than* / *lighter than* / *lighter that* yours.
2 I think headphones are *more useful* / *usefuller* / *useful more* than earbuds.
3 Gary's tablet is *biger* / *more big* / *bigger* than this one.
4 Our camera is *heavier* / *more heavy* / *heavyer* than theirs.
5 In my opinion, tablets are *difficulter* / *more difficult* / *difficult* to use than computers.
6 The camera on my new phone is *gooder* / *more good* / *better* than the camera on my old phone.
7 Texting my friends is *easier* / *more easy* / *easyer* than emailing them.
8 The traffic in New York is *worser* / *worse* / *badder* than the traffic in Chicago.

b Look at the information about the two TVs and complete the sentences. Use the comparative forms of the adjectives in the box.

Television	HiTek TV	PicX TV
1 Weight	20 kg	18 kg
2 Screen size	48 inches	55 inches
3 Picture quality	★★★★☆	★★★★★
4 Sound quality	★★★★☆	★★★☆☆
5 Easy to use?	★★★☆☆	★★★★★
6 Appearance	★★☆☆☆	★★★☆☆
7 First sold	December 2020	February 2022
8 Price	€550	€495

attractive   new   good   easy   expensive
~~heavy~~   clear   big

1 **Weight:** The HiTek TV is ___heavier___ than the PicX TV.
2 **Screen size:** The PicX TV is _____ than the HiTek TV.
3 **Picture quality:** The picture on the PicX TV is _____ than on the HiTek TV.
4 **Sound quality:** The sound is _____ on the HiTek TV than on the PicX TV.
5 **Easy to use?** The PicX TV is _____ to use than the HiTek TV.
6 **Appearance:** The PicX TV is _____ than the HiTek TV.
7 **First sold:** The PicX TV is _____ than the HiTek TV.
8 **Price:** The HiTek TV is _____ than the PicX TV.

2 VOCABULARY IT collocations

a Match 1–5 with a–e to make sentences.

1 [c] Click on
2 [ ] Enter your username and password to log into
3 [ ] Click here to download
4 [ ] He forgot to save
5 [ ] For more information about our products, visit

a our website or call this number.
b the document before closing down his computer.
c this link to watch our new video clip.
d powerful antivirus software. Keep your computer safe.
e the computers in this library.

b Underline the correct words to complete the sentences.

1 No, you can't *download* / *log into* my computer. It's private!
2 You can use my laptop to *check* / *visit* your email.
3 When you *save* / *visit* their website, they give a dollar to help poor people.
4 You should *check* / *save* your document every 15 minutes.
5 You can listen to her new song if you click on this *link* / *computer*.
6 Please don't download any unsafe *websites* / *files* to my computer.
7 I like to *go* / *click* online and watch videos.

58

10B | WHAT'S THE MOST BEAUTIFUL LANGUAGE IN THE WORLD?

1 GRAMMAR Superlative adjectives

a Underline the correct words to complete the sentences.

1 They say that Arabic is one of *the more difficult /* <u>*the most difficult*</u> */ the difficultest* languages *of the world / than the world /* <u>*in the world*</u>.

2 Spanish is one of *the most popular / most popular / the popularest* languages *for learn / to learn / for learning*.

3 I think Lionel Messi is *the goodest / the best / the most good* football player of all time.

4 I work in one of *the noisyest / the most noisy / the noisiest* areas *in the city / at the city / on the city*.

5 I think Xhosa is *the more strange / the strangest / the most strange* language! I heard people speaking it in South Africa.

6 I think Brazil is *the interestingest / most interesting / the most interesting* country to visit *in South America / of South America / by South America*.

7 The Internet is one of *the more useful / the most useful / the usefulest* inventions of the 20th century.

8 He's one of *the most famous / the famousest / the more famous* actors in Hollywood.

b Put the words in the correct order to make sentences.

1 funniest / one / of the / on TV / he's / people .
<u>He's one of the funniest people on TV.</u>

2 Japanese / languages / is / hardest / to learn / the / one of .
_____

3 the / Sam / best / in our class / student / is .
_____

4 was / the / day / wettest / last Tuesday / of the year .
_____

5 one of / beautiful / the / it's / buildings / most / in the world .
_____

6 is / the / which / city / biggest / in the world ?
_____

7 we / last year / the / had / winter / since 1986 / coldest .
_____

8 in the world / the / land animal / the cheetah / fastest / is .
_____

2 VOCABULARY High numbers

a Tick (✓) the correct words.

1 7,500
   a ☐ seven hundred and fifty
   b ✓ seven thousand five hundred
   c ☐ seven million five hundred thousand

2 812
   a ☐ eight twelve hundred
   b ☐ eight thousand and twelve
   c ☐ eight hundred and twelve

3 2,500,000
   a ☐ two million five hundred thousand
   b ☐ two thousand five hundred
   c ☐ twenty-five hundred thousand

4 1,299
   a ☐ twelve ninety-nine
   b ☐ one thousand, two hundred and ninety-nine
   c ☐ one million two hundred and ninety-nine thousand

5 2001
   a ☐ two thousand and one
   b ☐ twenty and one
   c ☐ two hundred and one

b ▶ 10.01 Listen and check.

c Write the numbers in words.

1 85,000,000   *eighty-five million* _____
2 379   _____
3 8,162   _____
4 450,000   _____
5 2009   _____
6 7,299,612   _____

3 PRONUNCIATION Main stress

a ▶ 10.02 Listen and decide where the main stress is in each superlative form. Tick (✓) the correct stress marking.

1 a ☐ English is the <u>most</u> popular language in the world.
  b ✓ English is the most <u>popular</u> language in the world.

2 a ☐ The Gambia is one of the <u>small</u>est countries in Africa.
  b ☐ The Gambia is one of the small<u>est</u> countries in Africa.

3 a ☐ This is one of the most <u>dangerous</u> cities in the world.
  b ☐ This is one of the <u>most</u> dangerous cities in the world.

4 a ☐ Brazil is the <u>biggest</u> country in Latin America.
  b ☐ Brazil is the <u>biggest</u> country in Latin America.

5 a ☐ Spanish is one of the most <u>useful</u> languages in the world.
  b ☐ Spanish is one of the <u>most</u> useful languages in the world.

6 a ☐ This is the <u>most</u> expensive restaurant in the city.
  b ☐ This is the most <u>expensive</u> restaurant in the city.

7 a ☐ This is one of the <u>saddest</u> films ever.
  b ☐ This is one of the sadd<u>est</u> films ever.

8 a ☐ This is the heav<u>iest</u> thing in my bag.
  b ☐ This is the <u>heav</u>iest thing in my bag.

10C EVERYDAY ENGLISH
There's something I don't know how to do

1 USEFUL LANGUAGE
Asking for help

a Complete the conversation with the words in the box.

> showing   not at all   like this   right   ~~could~~
> looks   so first   of course   easy

A ¹ <u>Could</u> you help me with something?

B Yes, ²_____. What is it?

A I don't know how to record programmes on my new TV.

B Right, that's ³_____.

A Would you mind ⁴_____ me?

B No, ⁵_____. So, what you do is this. First, you go to the programme menu, then you find the programme you want and, finally, you press 'Record'.

A OK, that ⁶_____ easy. Now let me try. ⁷_____ I go to the programme menu?

B Yes, that's right.

A Then I find the programme I want with these arrows, ⁸_____?

B Correct.

A And I just press the 'Record' button. Is that ⁹_____?

B Yes, perfect. Well done!

b ▶ 10.03 Listen and check.

c <u>Underline</u> the correct words to complete the sentences.

1. **A** Could you *helping / to help / <u>help</u>* me with my homework?
   B Yes, *of course / off course / course*.
2. Can you explain *me / that to me / that me*?
3. **A** Would you mind *help / helping / to help* me?
   B No, *not at all / not all / no at all*.
4. **A** Do you mind *show / to show / showing* me how to take photos with my phone?
   B *Not problem / No problem / Without a problem*.
5. *At first / First place / So first* I click on this link?
6. Next, I put in my password, *like this / as this / like these*?
7. And then I press this button. Is that *in right / right / on the right*?

d ▶ 10.04 Listen and check.

2 PRONUNCIATION
Main stress and intonation

a ▶ 10.05 Listen to the questions. Tick (✓) the stressed word in each sentence.

1. Can you help me with something?
   a ☐ can
   b ✓ help
2. Would you mind showing me how to do it?
   a ☐ showing
   b ☐ mind
3. Could you explain that again, please?
   a ☐ could
   b ☐ explain
4. Do you mind helping me with my shopping?
   a ☐ helping
   b ☐ mind

b ▶ 10.06 Listen to the questions. Put a tick (✓) to show if the intonation goes up (↗) or down (↘) at the end.

	↗	↘
1 How do I check my email?	☐	✓
2 Can you show me how to log in?	☐	☐
3 What's the problem with your computer?	☐	☐
4 Would you mind speaking more slowly, please?	☐	☐
5 Do you mind showing me how to take photos?	☐	☐
6 How often do you check your email?	☐	☐

10D | SKILLS FOR WRITING
My friends send really funny texts

1 READING

a On 'Compare the Web' you can compare different websites. Read people's opinions about two social media sites, Interfriends and BestiesLink. Who thinks these things? Use the names in the box.

| Joe K | ~~Enuff!~~ | Helpme2 | Lizzie39 |

1 I use the site to help me with my studies. <u>Enuff!</u>
2 My friends and I enjoy photography. _____
3 Social media isn't the best way to talk to people. _____
4 It's the best site to make plans with friends. _____

b Read the opinions again. Are the sentences true (*T*) or false (*F*)?

1 Joe K is quiet and doesn't like spending time with his friends.
2 Enuff! is a bad language student and never studies.
3 Helpme2 doesn't use social media very often.
4 Lizzie39 thinks social media sites are a bad idea.
5 More people prefer Interfriends to BestiesLink.

2 WRITING SKILLS Linking ideas with *also*, *too* and *as well*

a Rewrite the sentences. Add the words in brackets in the correct places.

1 He speaks Chinese perfectly and he speaks a little Japanese. (too)
   <u>He speaks Chinese perfectly and he speaks a little Japanese, too.</u>

2 My new tablet is smaller than my old laptop. It's lighter, so it's easier to carry. (also)
   _____
   _____

3 Put in your username and enter your password. (as well)
   _____
   _____

4 I can take great photos with my new phone, and I can post them on social media. (also)
   _____
   _____

5 He's got a new tablet and a new smartphone. (too)
   _____
   _____

6 My uncle gave me a laptop and he bought me a printer. (as well)
   _____
   _____

> 👤 For me, Interfriends is better than BestiesLink. You can put a lot of pictures on Interfriends and make bigger photo albums. Most of my friends use Interfriends as well, so it's easier to talk to them. We like to plan events and parties in group chats.
>
> **Joe K** Like | Reply | Share

> 👤 BestiesLink is the most famous social media site in my country, so of course it's the best. You can do more things on it, too. It's also a good site because you can use different apps on it. For example, my friends and I use a language learning app and study English together.
>
> **Enuff!** Like | Reply | Share

> 👤 I use Interfriends almost every day. It's quicker to share photos with friends than on BestiesLink, and I love taking pictures.
>
> **Helpme2** Like | Reply | Share

> 👤 I don't like Interfriends or BestiesLink. If I want to talk to my friends or show them photos, I can go to their house. My real friends are better than some people I only see on social media sites.
>
> **Lizzie39** Like | Reply | Share

3 WRITING

a Think of two websites you use that are similar. Write a post comparing them on 'Compare the Web'. Look at Joe K's post to help you. Remember to:

- say why you like one more than the other
- say what you use the better site for and why
- use *also*, *too* and *as well*.

> 👤 For me, _____ is better than
> _____
> _____
> _____
> _____
> _____
> _____
> _____
> _____
> _____
> _____
> _____
>
> Like | Reply | Share

1 READING

a Read the text. Complete each sentence with the correct tip number.

1 Tip __5__ talks about doing something for the first time.
2 Tip ____ talks about staying healthy.
3 Tip ____ talks about spending less time on your phone.
4 Tip ____ talks about spending time with the people who are important to you.
5 Tip ____ talks about being friendly.

b Read the text again. Match 1–8 with a–h to make sentences.

1 [g] Checking emails often takes
2 ☐ Getting fit can help
3 ☐ Doing exercise is
4 ☐ It's important not to forget
5 ☐ Many of us spend
6 ☐ It's a good idea to
7 ☐ When you are nice to other people,
8 ☐ Helping other people

a a lot of time on social media.
b about your family and friends.
c can be good for you.
d try new and different things sometimes.
e good for your brain.
f they are usually nice to you.
g too much of our time.
h you to feel happier.

c What other things do you think are important for a happy life? Write some more tips. Remember to write:

- what the tip is
- how often someone should do this
- how it will make them feel better.

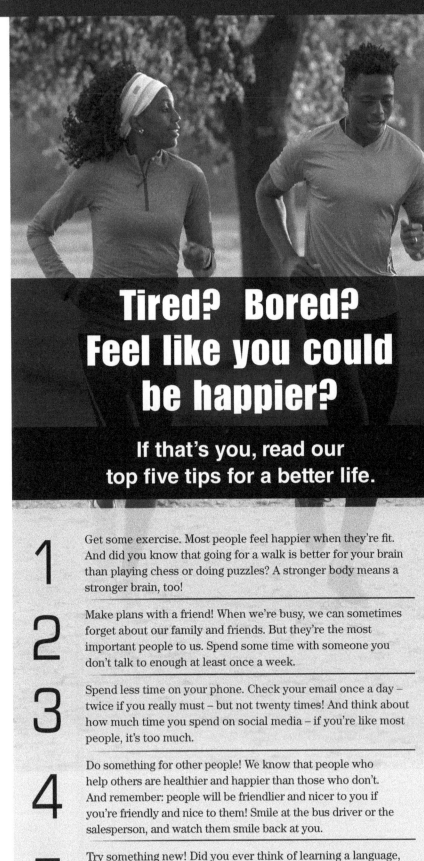

Tired? Bored? Feel like you could be happier?

If that's you, read our top five tips for a better life.

1 Get some exercise. Most people feel happier when they're fit. And did you know that going for a walk is better for your brain than playing chess or doing puzzles? A stronger body means a stronger brain, too!

2 Make plans with a friend! When we're busy, we can sometimes forget about our family and friends. But they're the most important people to us. Spend some time with someone you don't talk to enough at least once a week.

3 Spend less time on your phone. Check your email once a day – twice if you really must – but not twenty times! And think about how much time you spend on social media – if you're like most people, it's too much.

4 Do something for other people! We know that people who help others are healthier and happier than those who don't. And remember: people will be friendlier and nicer to you if you're friendly and nice to them! Smile at the bus driver or the salesperson, and watch them smile back at you.

5 Try something new! Did you ever think of learning a language, trying a new sport or playing the piano? Well, don't just think about it – do it! It's probably easier than you think.

For more ideas, visit our website.

2 LISTENING

a **10.07** Listen to the podcast. Tick (✓) the best description of what the person says.

1. ☐ People who live in Blue Zones live longer and are near oceans, rivers and lakes.
2. ☐ People who live in Blue Zones live longer and eat a lot of meat.
3. ☐ People who live in Blue Zones live longer and do some exercise.

b Complete the sentences about the podcast. Use numbers (e.g., *300*), not words (e.g., *three hundred*).

1. In 2019, there were about ___*80,000*___ people over 100.
2. In 2014, there were _____ Americans aged 100 or older.
3. Blue Zones are places that have the highest number of people _____ years old or older.
4. Both coffee and tea drinkers are in _____ percent less danger of an early death.
5. Keep a healthy social network. This can help you live up to _____ percent longer.
6. _____ close friends in your social network may lower the danger of early death.

c ▶ **10.07** Listen to the podcast again. Are the sentences true (*T*) or false (*F*)?

1. The number of Americans 100 years old is bigger now.
2. The people who live in Loma Linda eat sugar, dance and watch TV.
3. The people in Costa Rica feel good about life.
4. Okinawa is the home of the world's oldest men.
5. Eight hours is not enough sleep.

⊙ Review and extension

1 GRAMMAR

Correct the sentences.

1. My new computer is more fast than my old one.
   My new computer is faster than my old one.
2. Tablets are usually lighter that laptops.
3. London is the most big city in the UK.
4. This hotel is cheapper than the Hotel Classic.
5. It's the more expensive restaurant in the world.
6. Spanish is more easy to learn than Navajo.
7. English is the most useful language of the world.
8. I'm not very good at maths, but Bilal is badder than me.

2 VOCABULARY

Correct the sentences.

1. There was nothing good on TV, so I go on social media after dinner.
   There was nothing good on TV, so I went on social media after dinner.
2. I use my smartphone to do calls to my family and friends.
3. I online to check the weather.
4. You need my password to log to my computer.
5. Press "Control" and "S" when you want to safe your document.
6. It's taking a long time to inload the file from this website.

3 WORDPOWER *most*

Choose the correct words to complete the sentences.

1. I felt ill yesterday, so I was in bed *most day / most of the day / most of day*.
2. They love watching all kinds of sport, but they like tennis *most of all / most all / most everything*.
3. *Most friends mine / Most my friends / Most of my friends* live in Thailand.
4. I think *most people / most the people / most of people* like listening to music.
5. *Most the students / Most of the students / Most of students* in my class speak excellent English.
6. We visit my grandparents *most of Sundays / most of the Sundays / most Sundays*.

↻ REVIEW YOUR PROGRESS

Look again at Review your progress on p. 108 of the Student's Book. How well can you do these things now?
3 = very well   2 = well   1 = not so well

I CAN ...	
compare and talk about things I have	☐
talk about languages	☐
ask for help	☐
write a post expressing an opinion.	☐

1 GRAMMAR Present perfect

a Complete the sentences with the present perfect form of the verbs in the box.

see go act do try read dance ~~meet~~

1 __Have__ you ever __met__ a famous football player?
2 Gina _____ _____ the film *Avengers: Endgame* four times!
3 David and Max _____ never _____ any of the Harry Potter books.
4 No, he _____ _____ in a Shakespeare play before.
5 We _____ never _____ Japanese food.
6 I _____ never _____ the tango before.
7 No, I _____ _____ a bungee jump before, so I'm really nervous.
8 _____ your mother ever _____ to Australia or New Zealand?

b Put the words in the correct order to make sentences.

1 ever / have / heard of / you / the Spanish actor / Paz Vega ?
Have you ever heard of the Spanish actor, Paz Vega?
2 won / never / Tom Cruise / has / an Oscar .
_____
3 written / has / ever / she / any songs / in Italian ?
_____
4 to Dubai / we / been / have / before / never .
_____
5 in an orchestra / ever / have / Jun-ho and Grace / played ?
_____
6 never / I / have / before / a film star / met .
_____
7 had / you / have / a birthday party / ever / in a restaurant ?
_____
8 the Tower of London / have / never / they / visited .
_____

2 VOCABULARY
Irregular past participles

a Find the irregular past participles for the verbs in the box.

~~see~~ win eat have break catch meet
do hear buy make steal write read

Q	H	X	E	N	I	S	F	G	B	D	E	F	G	L
H	Z	F	B	F	H	J	K	E	R	E	A	X	G	K
H	F	M	X	E	J	L	R	Z	O	S	W	R	R	C
E	A	T	E	N	A	N	E	M	K	S	O	G	N	A
A	I	A	H	B	C	D	A	S	E	G	N	N	S	U
R	F	B	F	G	H	A	D	D	N	N	G	S	D	G
D	F	P	R	W	E	F	H	V	F	D	S	U	U	H
B	G	D	Y	O	Y	U	F	B	J	S	S	D	F	T
F	E	H	O	I	A	D	H	J	V	T	V	E	G	G
H	S	E	E	N	P	D	F	B	B	O	U	G	H	T
P	H	H	G	F	E	M	A	G	N	L	K	D	V	R
D	H	L	Y	U	U	A	Q	D	F	E	L	F	D	A
S	Z	A	A	L	O	D	W	D	F	N	R	M	Z	I
F	W	R	I	T	T	E	N	F	G	H	D	D	E	Q
U	T	T	D	F	J	N	G	S	X	U	X	Q	E	T

b Complete the past participles in the sentences.

1 Have you ever b__een__ to Spain?
2 *The Godfather* is the best film I've ever s_____.
3 I've never w_____ a competition.
4 My brother's b_____ his arm three times.
5 Have you ever e_____ an unusual dish?
6 He's w_____ a lot of magazine articles.
7 My father has r_____ thousands of books.
8 We've never b_____ a house.

3 PRONUNCIATION Main stress

a ▶11.01 Listen to the sentences and tick (✓) the correct stress marking.

1 a ☐ <u>I've</u> never read any novels by Ernest Hemingway.
  b ✓ I've never <u>read</u> any novels by Ernest Hemingway.
2 a ☐ <u>Have</u> you ever stayed in that hotel?
  b ☐ Have you ever <u>stayed</u> in that hotel?
3 a ☐ He's <u>driven</u> to Paris six times this year.
  b ☐ <u>He's</u> driven to Paris six times this year.
4 a ☐ Ella and Greg have never <u>met</u> you.
  b ☐ Ella and Greg <u>have</u> never met you.
5 a ☐ <u>Have</u> you ever bought a new car?
  b ☐ Have you ever <u>bought</u> a new car?
6 a ☐ She hasn't <u>met</u> the president before.
  b ☐ She <u>hasn't</u> met the president before.

11B I BET YOU'VE NEVER BEEN TO THE OPERA

1 GRAMMAR
Present perfect or past simple

a Match questions 1–6 with answers a–f.

1 [e] Has he ever won an Oscar?
2 [ ] Did you go on holiday last year?
3 [ ] How many times have you visited Venice?
4 [ ] Did you do anything special this weekend?
5 [ ] Have they ever been to a musical on Broadway?
6 [ ] Did she enjoy her birthday party?

a I've only been there once, in 2015.
b No, not really. We just went out for a pizza on Saturday night.
c Yes, they have, actually. They saw the play *Hamilton* when they were in New York last month.
d Yes, she did. She had a fantastic time.
e Yes, he has. He got one for his first film a few years ago.
f Yes, we did. We went to Cancún in Mexico.

b Underline the correct words to complete the conversation.

A ¹*Have you ever been / Did you ever go* to London?
B Yes, I ²*have / did*. I ³*'ve stayed / stayed* there lots of times on business.
A ⁴*Have you ever seen / Did you ever see* any musicals in the West End?
B No, I ⁵*didn't / haven't*. However, I ⁶*went / 've been* to the theatre a few times.
A Really? What ⁷*have you seen / did you see* the last time you went?
B I ⁸*saw / have seen* Shakespeare's *Romeo and Juliet* at The Globe Theatre last summer.
A Who ⁹*have you been / did you go* with?
B I ¹⁰*went / have been* with some English friends.
A ¹¹*Have you enjoyed it / Did you enjoy it*?
B Yes, I ¹²*have / did*. The acting ¹³*was / has been* great!

2 VOCABULARY Music

a Underline the correct words to match the pictures.

1 *a DJ / a musician*

2 *an opera singer / a pop singer*

3 *a classical dancer / a jazz musician*

4 *a rock band / a classical orchestra*

5 *tango DJs / tango dancers*

6 *a rock band / an opera*

b Complete the sentences.

1 Carlos Acosta was a famous ballet ___dancer___. He is now a director.
2 I think Pavarotti was the best opera _____ of his generation.
3 He's an amazing _____. He can play the piano, the guitar and the cello.
4 Suna's a violinist in one of the best-known _____ in Turkey.
5 They're probably the most popular South Korean boy _____. Their music videos have millions of views on YouTube.
6 My parents love _____ music, especially Beethoven and Tchaikovsky.
7 My grandfather loved _____ music. His favourite singer was Bob Dylan.
8 On the radio, they usually play _____ music by artists like Taylor Swift and Ariana Grande.
9 Louis Armstrong was a popular _____ singer. He also played the trumpet.
10 The Rolling Stones is one of the most famous _____ bands in the world.

3 PRONUNCIATION Syllables

a ▶11.02 Listen to the sentences. Which syllable is stressed in the **bold** words? Tick (✓) the correct stress marking.

1 He's a brilliant **actor**.
  a [ ] <u>ac</u>tor
  b [✓] ac<u>tor</u>

2 She's a famous Hollywood film **director**.
  a [ ] <u>di</u>rector
  b [ ] direc<u>tor</u>

3 I went to the **theatre** in London last night.
  a [ ] <u>thea</u>tre
  b [ ] thea<u>tre</u>

4 She was a well-known **model** when she was young.
  a [ ] <u>mo</u>del
  b [ ] mo<u>del</u>

5 I'd like to be a fashion **photographer**.
  a [ ] pho<u>tog</u>rapher
  b [ ] photogra<u>pher</u>

6 She's won several **national** prizes.
  a [ ] <u>na</u>tional
  b [ ] na<u>tional</u>

7 He's the best **musician** in our family.
  a [ ] <u>mu</u>sician
  b [ ] mu<u>si</u>cian

8 The **orchestra** played for three hours.
  a [ ] or<u>ches</u>tra
  b [ ] <u>or</u>chestra

1 USEFUL LANGUAGE
Asking for and expressing opinions

a Complete the conversation with the sentences in the box.

Yes, I thought it was great.
No, me neither. Anyway, let's go for a coffee.
~~I really liked the film. How about you?~~
Really? I thought the music was fine. Also, I thought the photography was great.
Yeah, maybe.

TIM So what did you think of the film?
SAM ¹ <u>I really liked the film. How about you?</u>
TIM I thought it was quite good, but it was a bit long.
SAM ² _____
TIM Did you like the music?
SAM ³ _____
TIM Did you? I thought it was a bit loud. Sometimes I couldn't hear the actors very well.
SAM ⁴ _____
TIM Yes, me too. But I didn't like the actor who was Nelson Mandela.
SAM ⁵ _____

b ▶11.03 Listen and check.

c Correct the sentences.

1 **A** What have you thought of the concert?
   What did you think of the concert?
   B I really like it.
2 **A** Did you enjoyed the film?
   B Yes, I was. I thinked the acting was excellent.
3 **A** I didn't like very much the singer.
   B Me, too.
4 **A** I've thought the music was lovely.
   B Yes, me also.
5 **A** I have really enjoyed the concert last night. How are you?
   B I haven't liked the first half at all, but the second half has been amazing.

2 PRONUNCIATION
Main stress and intonation

a ▶11.04 Listen to the short conversations. Put a tick (✓) to show if B's responses go up (↗) or down (↘).

		↗	↘
1 **A** I thought the film was brilliant.			
B Did you		✓	☐
2 **A** I really liked the music.			
B Me too.		☐	☐
3 **A** I love going to the theatre.			
B Do you?		☐	☐
4 **A** I didn't like Tom Cruise's last film.			
B Me neither.		☐	☐

11D SKILLS FOR WRITING
It was an interesting film

1 READING

a Mariusz, from Poland, and Ariel, from Argentina, both went to see the band Flags in their hometowns. Read their messages to each other about the concerts and tick (✓) the correct answers.

1 Who thought the concert was terrible?
   a ☐ Mariusz   b ☐ Ariel
2 Who thought the concert was really good?
   a ☐ Mariusz   b ☐ Ariel

Hi Ariel,

How are you? I hope your family is well.

I wanted to write and tell you about the Flags concert I went to last weekend. It was fantastic! I loved every minute of it. I went with a big group of friends from university. It was really crazy, but a lot of fun! The singer had an amazing voice, and the band played all their songs. The members of the band talked to everyone, too. They were really nice and very friendly. I'd love to see them again.

If you visit me in Poland next year, maybe we can go and see them on their next tour. What do you think?

See you,

Mariusz

Hey Mariusz,

Great to hear from you! My family and I are all well. Thanks for asking. Come and visit us again any time!

So, you enjoyed the Flags concert, did you? I'm surprised. I saw them at the stadium here in Mendoza a few months ago, and I didn't like them at all. I went with my sister for her birthday. (She really likes the singer!) I thought the music was terrible. It was too loud!

And when the band talked to the crowd, it was so boring. I didn't go to a concert to listen to four men talking! Thanks for the invitation, but I don't want to see them again!

When I visit you in Poland, we can see a different band that we both like!

See you,

Ariel

b Read the messages again. Are the sentences true (*T*) or false (*F*)?

1 Mariusz went to the concert with his family.
2 Flags played all their songs at the concert Mariusz went to.
3 The band only played music at the concerts.
4 Flags sang at the concert hall in Ariel's town.
5 Ariel doesn't want to see Flags with Mariusz.

2 WRITING SKILLS Object pronouns

a Rewrite the sentences. Change the **bold** words to object pronouns to avoid repetition.

1 I read Jane Austen's *Emma* last week. I really loved **Jane Austen's *Emma***.
I read Jane Austen's *Emma* last week. I really loved it.
2 Tom Hardy was my favourite actor in the film. **Tom Hardy** was really good.

3 We want to see the new Marvel film. My friend, Leo, told us **the new Marvel film** is amazing.
4 Alfonso Cuarón is a fantastic director. **Alfonso Cuarón** won an Oscar for the film *Roma*.
5 I thought Jay-Z and Beyoncé were fantastic in concert. **Jay-Z and Beyoncé** are both great artists.

3 WRITING

a Think of a concert you've been to, a film you've seen or a book you've read. Write a message to a friend and tell them your opinions about it. Remember to write:

- when you went / saw it / read it
- if you liked it, or not
- your opinions about the singer / actor / main character, etc.
- if you recommend it.

1 READING

a Read the text and <u>underline</u> the correct words to complete the sentences.

1 Lisa Kudrow *works* / <u>*worked*</u> as a scientist.
2 Lisa studied *biology* / *acting* at university.
3 Lisa was *a producer* / *an actor* in the TV series *Friends*.
4 Lisa and her husband have a *son* / *daughter*.
5 Lisa *is* / *was* an actor, writer and producer.

b Read the text again. Complete the sentences with the correct form of the verbs in the box.

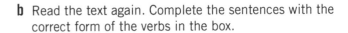

~~play~~ win study be earn live act

1 Lisa Kudrow ____played____ tennis in high school.
2 Lisa and Michel _____ in Los Angeles now.
3 She _____ in many popular TV programmes.
4 Lisa _____ biology at university.
5 The actors _____ a lot of money for working on *Friends*.
6 Lisa _____ an actor for many years.
7 She _____ awards for her excellent work in TV programmes and films.

c Write a profile of a famous person. Make sure you include at least three verbs in the present perfect form.

Celebrity Profile

Lisa Kudrow is a famous actor who has won several awards, including an Emmy. She has played some great characters in TV programmes and in films, but she hasn't always been an actor. Before she became a famous actor, Lisa was an athlete and a scientist.

Lisa grew up in California. When she was in high school, Lisa was a great student and an excellent tennis player. Her father was a doctor who helped people with headaches, and her mother was a travel agent. Lisa went to university in New York and earned a biology degree. After university, she worked as a medical researcher for her father.

Lisa left her job and soon got the role of Phoebe Buffay in the popular TV series *Friends*. The series became so famous that Lisa and her co-stars earned over $1 million for each episode! She became a big star and has acted in many films and TV series since *Friends*. She is also a writer and a producer. She has worked as a producer for TV programmes like *Who Do You Think You Are?* and *Web Therapy*.

Lisa lives in Los Angeles. She married Michel Stern in 1995, and they had a son named Julian in 1998. Since Julian was born, Lisa has acted in several films for children, such as *Hotel for Dogs* and *The Boss Baby*. Lisa Kudrow is a very clever celebrity who has had an amazing life!

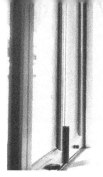

2 LISTENING

a ▶ 11.05 Listen to the conversation. Tick (✓) the things Marianne and Lenny talk about.

☐ places they have been to   ☐ food they have eaten
☐ famous people they have met   ☐ films they have seen
☐ stories they have read   ☐ music they enjoy

b ▶ 11.05 Listen to the conversation again and tick (✓) the correct answers.

1 Why does Lenny like Mexico?
   a ☐ He likes the history, the music and the food.
   b ✓ He likes the history, the beaches and the food.
   c ☐ He likes the history, the beaches and the weather.

2 Why doesn't Marianne want to try Mexican food?
   a ☐ She doesn't eat meat.
   b ☐ She doesn't like beans.
   c ☐ She's never been to Mexico.

3 Why does Marianne like Bologna so much?
   a ☐ She met Lenny there.
   b ☐ She's seen operas there.
   c ☐ She's had good food there.

4 How much Italian does Marianne speak?
   a ☐ A lot. She learned it at school.
   b ☐ None. She's forgotten all of it.
   c ☐ Not much. She's forgotten most of it.

5 What has Marianne seen in Milan?
   a ☐ Italian operas
   b ☐ pop singers
   c ☐ classical music concerts

6 Why does Marianne already know about the band Arctic Fire?
   a ☐ Because she went to one of their concerts.
   b ☐ Because her brother has some of their albums.
   c ☐ Because her friend in Italy likes them.

7 What does Marianne think you need to do to enjoy classical music?
   a ☐ Go to concerts.
   b ☐ Listen to it more than one time.
   c ☐ Like different kinds of music.

8 What often happens when Lenny buys pop albums?
   a ☐ He likes one song best at first, and it stays his favourite song.
   b ☐ When he has listened several times, he gets bored with it.
   c ☐ He likes one song best at first, then starts to like other songs more.

c Write about the things you enjoy in your life. Start with these topics and add two of your own:

- What's the nicest food you've eaten?
- What's the most interesting place you've been?
- What's the best present anyone has bought for you?

For each topic, describe the thing you have chosen and explain why you liked it.

 # Review and extension

1 GRAMMAR

Correct the sentences.

1 Have you never met a famous pop singer?
   Have you ever met a famous pop singer?
2 I never seen a film by Wes Anderson.
3 They has never been to Canberra.
4 I haven't never been to Turkey on holiday.
5 My uncle has write lots of children's books.
6 Have ever you read any of the Harry Potter books?
7 **A** Has he ever been to Scotland?
   B No, he never.
8 I'm visited my grandmother three times this week.

2 VOCABULARY

Correct the sentences.

1 My dad's ben to Colombia seven times.
   My dad's been to Colombia seven times.
2 I've never forgetted your birthday.
3 No, I've never flied in a helicopter.
4 Have they maken a new James Bond film?
5 I've taked lots of photos of the party.
6 No, I've never takken the bus to school. I always walk.

3 WORDPOWER Multi-word verbs

Complete the sentences with the multi-word verbs. Use one word from each line.

come	try	grew	call	fill	~~lies~~
over	on	~~down~~	up	back	in

1 My father always ___lies___ ___down___ on the sofa when he's watching TV. He usually falls asleep.
2 I _____ _____ in South Korea, but I went to university in Japan.
3 Sorry, he isn't here at the moment. I'll ask him to _____ you _____.
4 If you _____ _____ at about 8:00, we can watch the football match on my new 3D TV.
5 If you want to join the gym, first you have to _____ _____ this application form.
6 Why don't you _____ these jeans _____?

REVIEW YOUR PROGRESS

Look again at Review your progress on p. 118 of the Student's Book. How well can you do these things now?
3 = very well   2 = well   1 = not so well

I CAN ...	
ask and answer about entertainment experiences	☐
talk about events I've been to	☐
ask for and express opinions about things I've seen	☐
write a review.	☐

1 VOCABULARY Geography

a Complete the crossword puzzle.

→ **Across**

3 The Amazon is the longest ___river___ in South America.
6 Scientists are very worried about the animals and trees in the Amazon _____ in Brazil.
8 A _____ is a huge area of ice millions of years old that moves very slowly down a mountain valley.
9 When I go on holiday to the coast, I don't like lying on the _____ all day.
10 A _____ is a large body of fresh water with land all around it.

↓ **Down**

1 Cuba is one of the largest _____ in the Caribbean.
2 The sequoias are the largest trees in the world, and you can see them in a huge _____ in California.
4 Angel Falls is one of the highest _____ in the world.
5 Everest is the tallest _____ in the world.
7 Death Valley is in the Mojave _____ in Eastern California. It is one of the hottest places on Earth.

2 GRAMMAR *be going to*

a Match questions 1–6 with answers a–f.

1 [e] Are you going to stay in a hotel?
2 [ ] What are you going to do in Indonesia?
3 [ ] Is she going to go to university next year?
4 [ ] How are you going to save enough money to travel?
5 [ ] Are they going to stay with their uncle in Madrid?
6 [ ] Are you going to catch the bus to the airport?

a No, she isn't going to continue studying. She's going to get a job as a tour guide in Mexico.
b We're going to work in a big hotel in Marmaris for six months.
c Yes, they are. He's going to get them a job in a restaurant while they are there.
d No, we aren't. We're going to call a taxi at about 4 o'clock.
e No, we aren't. We're going to go camping.
f We're going to go hiking in the mountains.

b Complete the sentences with the verbs in the box and the correct form of *be going to*. Use contractions where possible.

---
visit   (not) go   stay   look   (not) have   come   ~~do~~   have
---

1 What ___are___ you _going to do_ this weekend?
2 He _____ a holiday this year because he bought a new car.
3 We _____ the Sydney Opera House while we're in Australia.
4 Which hotel _____ you _____ at when you're in Chicago?
5 _____ she _____ for a job in Kyoto?
6 _____ you _____ a big party for your thirtieth birthday?
7 I _____ to the beach this afternoon. It looks like it's going to rain.
8 They _____ over to watch the World Cup on TV with us this evening.

3 PRONUNCIATION
Syllables and word stress

a ▶12.01 Listen to the sentences. Which syllable is stressed in the **bold** words? Tick (✓) the correct stress marking.

1 In London, the **accommodation** is really expensive.
  a [✓] accommo<u>da</u>tion   b [ ] acc<u>o</u>mmodation
2 I've done a lot of **sightseeing** today.
  a [ ] sight<u>see</u>ing   b [ ] <u>sight</u>seeing
3 I like living in the **countryside**.
  a [ ] <u>coun</u>tryside   b [ ] country<u>side</u>
4 We have a **reservation** for 7:30.
  a [ ] reser<u>va</u>tion   b [ ] <u>re</u>servation
5 The **nightlife** in Barcelona was brilliant.
  a [ ] <u>night</u>life   b [ ] night<u>life</u>
6 I love **travelling** to different countries.
  a [ ] <u>tra</u>velling   b [ ] trave<u>lling</u>
7 That **restaurant** has fantastic food.
  a [ ] restau<u>rant</u>   b [ ] <u>res</u>taurant
8 The **scenery** in Switzerland was amazing.
  a [ ] <u>sce</u>nery   b [ ] sce<u>ne</u>ry

1 GRAMMAR should / shouldn't

a Underline the best words to complete the sentences.

1 You *should / shouldn't* do some research before you go, so you know the best places to visit.
2 You *should / shouldn't* change your money at the airport. It's better to change it at a bank.
3 You *should / shouldn't* phone your parents every two or three days, so they know you're safe.
4 You *should / shouldn't* book some accommodation before you travel. Hotels are often full this time of the year.
5 You *should / shouldn't* speak too loudly to the local people. They might think it's rude.
6 You *should / shouldn't* learn some useful expressions in the local language. People like it when visitors can say a few words in their language.
7 You *should / shouldn't* spend too much time in the sun. It's very strong at this time of the year.
8 You *should / shouldn't* carry a lot of cash with you. It's safer to get money from cash machines when you need it.

b Correct the sentences.

1 You shouldn't to take so many jumpers with you on holiday.
   You shouldn't take so many jumpers with you on holiday.
2 She don't should walk home alone. It's safer to go by taxi.
   _____
3 You should seeing the new X-Men film. It's amazing!
   _____
4 Where I should change my money?
   _____
5 Which countries do I should visit in South America?
   _____
6 My dad thinks I should going to university next year.
   _____
7 They should to go to the toy museum when they're in Istanbul.
   _____
8 I should invite Selena and her sister to the party?
   _____

2 VOCABULARY Travel collocations

a Match 1–6 with a–f to make sentences.

1 [c] The first thing I do when I get to my hotel is to unpack
2 [ ] Elena and Carla are making
3 [ ] On holidays, my wife prefers to stay in
4 [ ] I think teachers are very lucky because they can often go on
5 [ ] We haven't got enough money for a holiday this year, so we're going to stay at
6 [ ] I think you should live

a hotels, but I think it's more fun to go camping.
b home and invite some friends to come and stay with us.
c my suitcase and put all my clothes in the wardrobe.
d abroad if you want to learn to speak a foreign language well.
e plans to go travelling around Asia for six months.
f a long summer holiday.

b Complete the sentences with the correct form of the verbs in the box.

plan   stay   ~~change~~   book   travel   pack

1 She says she can't come to the party tonight because she had to ___*change*___ her plans.
2 I _____ a holiday in Cambodia, but I couldn't go because of my sister's wedding.
3 It always takes her about six hours to _____ her bags before she goes on holiday.
4 We _____ the hotel in January, but now they say we haven't got a reservation.
5 He usually _____ abroad six or seven times a year.
6 There weren't any flights to Washington, D.C. that day because the weather was bad, so they _____ at home.

3 PRONUNCIATION Sound and spelling: /l/

a ▶12.02 Listen to the sentences. Is there a /l/ sound in the words in **bold**? Tick (✓) the correct answers.

	Yes	No
1 It was too **cold** to swim in the sea.	✓	
2 **Would** you like to have lunch in a café?		
3 You **should** visit the Science Museum.		
4 You should try the **grilled** fish – it's amazing!		
5 You can **walk** to the theatre from the station.		
6 The **oldest** building is the 14th-century castle.		

12C | EVERYDAY ENGLISH
Is breakfast included?

1 USEFUL LANGUAGE
Checking in at a hotel; Asking for tourist information

a Put the conversation between a guest (G) and a hotel receptionist (R) in the correct order.

- [ ] **G** Henderson.
- [ ] **G** Great. Oh, what time is breakfast?
- [ ] **R** Yes, there is. It's on the top floor next to the spa.
- [1] **R** Hello. How can I help you?
- [ ] **G** And what time is check-out?
- [ ] **R** It's from seven until ten in the dining room.
- [ ] **G** Thanks.
- [ ] **G** I've got a reservation for three nights.
- [ ] **G** Oh, and one last thing. Is there a gym I can use?
- [ ] **R** It's free of charge for our guests.
- [ ] **R** It's at 12 o'clock on the day you leave.
- [ ] **R** So here's your key. Enjoy your stay.
- [ ] **R** Three nights? Your name, please?
- [ ] **R** Thank you. Yes, that's right … Henderson. A single room for three nights.
- [ ] **G** How much does it cost to use the gym?
- [ ] **G** OK, that's great.

b ▶ 12.03 Listen and check.

c Match sentences 1–8 with responses a–h.

1 [e] I've won a holiday in Thailand!
2 [ ] Can I buy tickets here?
3 [ ] Is breakfast included?
4 [ ] I saw Jennifer Lawrence in a café yesterday!
5 [ ] Could I have four tickets, please?
6 [ ] Can I pay by credit card?
7 [ ] She's going to get her husband a cat for his birthday.
8 [ ] How much is it for a ticket?

a It's £10 for adults and £6 for children.
b Sure. That's £32, please.
c Of course. Please insert your card here.
d Oh, really? I didn't know Aydan liked animals.
e Have you? Wow! That's fantastic!
f Did you? Did you talk to her?
g Yes, it is. It's from 6:30 to 9:30 in the restaurant.
h Yes, you can. They're €20 each.

d ▶ 12.04 Listen and check.

2 PRONUNCIATION
Intonation to show surprise

a ▶ 12.05 Listen to the short conversations. Put a tick (✓) to show if B's responses go up (↗) or down (↘).

		↗	↘
1	**A** I've won £1,000!		
	B Oh, really?	✓	[ ]
2	**A** Thanks for all your help.		
	B No problem.	[ ]	[ ]
3	**A** I'm hungry.		
	B Me too. When's breakfast?	[ ]	[ ]
4	**A** I've missed the last train.		
	B Have you?	[ ]	[ ]
5	**A** I went to Rome for the weekend.		
	B Did you?	[ ]	[ ]
6	**A** Can you call me a taxi, please?		
	B Certainly.	[ ]	[ ]
7	**A** There's a car park under the hotel.		
	B How much is it?	[ ]	[ ]
8	**A** She's going to live in the USA.		
	B Is she?	[ ]	[ ]
9	**A** I really like opera.		
	B Do you?	[ ]	[ ]
10	**A** There's a really good café near my house.		
	B What time does it open?	[ ]	[ ]

12D | SKILLS FOR WRITING
You should explore the River Douro

1 READING

a Read Antonio and Gianni's emails and tick (✓) the best answer.

1. ☐ Antonio and Ana are going to go to Florence for a short holiday.
2. ☐ Antonio is going to stay at Gianni's house in Florence.
3. ☐ Antonio wants some information about where he should go in Florence.
4. ☐ Antonio has visited Florence before.

b Read the emails again. Are the sentences true (*T*) or false (*F*)?

1. Antonio wants to know about interesting places to visit and good places to eat.
2. *Il Ponte Vecchio* is the name of an expensive shop in Florence.
3. The statue of *David* is in the Uffizi Gallery.
4. The *Piazza della Signoria* is a great place to have a coffee.
5. Gianni doesn't like the food at *Il Santo Bevitore*.
6. Gianni would like to meet Antonio while he is in Florence.

2 WRITING SKILLS Paragraph writing

a Read the sentences. Put them in the correct order to make an email with an opening line, four paragraphs, and a closing line.

1. ☐ Secondly, you should go to the Royal Ontario Museum. It has an amazing collection of objects from all over the world.
2. ☐ I hope my ideas help you. Perhaps we can meet when you come to Toronto.
3. ☐ Thanks for your email.
4. ☐ You asked me about some interesting places to visit in Toronto, so here are some ideas.
5. ☐ Finally, the third place you should visit is the Art Gallery of Ontario. It is a great place to see paintings by Canadian artists.
6. ☐ You said you want to do some kind of sports activity. In December there are a lot of ice-skating rinks in Toronto, so you can go ice skating. It's great fun!
7. ☐ I'm pleased you're going to come to Toronto in December. I'm very happy to help you plan your trip.
8. ☐ Hi Edna,
9. ☐ Best wishes,
10. ☐ First, you should visit Casa Loma. It's a large castle with beautiful gardens.

3 WRITING

a Read Kenji's email and write a reply about a city or town you've visited. Think about:

- two or three places to visit
- why these places are interesting
- which places Kenji would like (read his email carefully)
- how to use paragraphs in your reply.

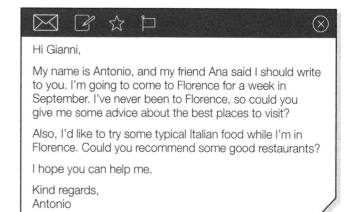

Hi Gianni,

My name is Antonio, and my friend Ana said I should write to you. I'm going to come to Florence for a week in September. I've never been to Florence, so could you give me some advice about the best places to visit?

Also, I'd like to try some typical Italian food while I'm in Florence. Could you recommend some good restaurants?

I hope you can help me.

Kind regards,
Antonio

Hi Antonio,

Thanks for your email. It's great that you're going to come to my home town in September. I'm very happy to help you plan your holiday.

You asked me about places to visit in Florence, so here are some ideas. First, you should visit the old bridge. We call it *Il Ponte Vecchio*. It's in the historic centre of Florence and there are lots of shops on the bridge where you can buy presents. The shops are quite expensive, but it's a beautiful place to begin a tour of Florence. Secondly, you should go to the Accademia Gallery. Here you can see Michelangelo's *David*. It's one of the most famous statues in the world. Finally, the third place you should go to is the Uffizi Gallery. It's got an amazing collection of Renaissance paintings. It's near a lovely square called the *Piazza della Signoria*. There are some nice cafés in the square where you can enjoy an excellent cup of Italian coffee.

You also asked me about restaurants. My favourite is *Il Santo Bevitore*. All the food there is fantastic!

I hope my ideas are useful. Maybe we can meet when you come to Florence!

Best wishes,

Gianni

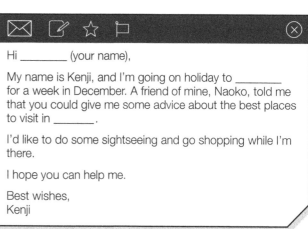

Hi _____ (your name),

My name is Kenji, and I'm going on holiday to _____ for a week in December. A friend of mine, Naoko, told me that you could give me some advice about the best places to visit in _____ .

I'd like to do some sightseeing and go shopping while I'm there.

I hope you can help me.

Best wishes,
Kenji

1 READING

a Read the emails. Match 1–4 with a–d to make sentences.

1. [d] Sarah is busy because
2. [ ] Sarah asks Maggie
3. [ ] Maggie thinks Sarah and her sister
4. [ ] Maggie tells Sarah that

a shouldn't book a hotel.
b they should stay with friends.
c what she should plan for her sister.
d she is planning a holiday.

b Read the emails again. Are these sentences true (*T*) or false (*F*)?

1. It is Sarah's birthday next month.
2. Sarah's sister wants to go on holiday and travel abroad.
3. Sarah wants to celebrate her sister's birthday abroad.
4. Maggie says that Sarah's sister should stay at home if that's what she wants.
5. Maggie says that Sarah should plan a different kind of holiday.
6. Maggie would like to know what Sarah thinks of her idea.

c Write an email to a friend about a problem. For example:

- a problem with a friend
- a problem at work
- a problem about a holiday
- your own idea.

d Write an email with an answer to the problem in c. Remember to write:

- what the person *should do*
- what the person *shouldn't do*.

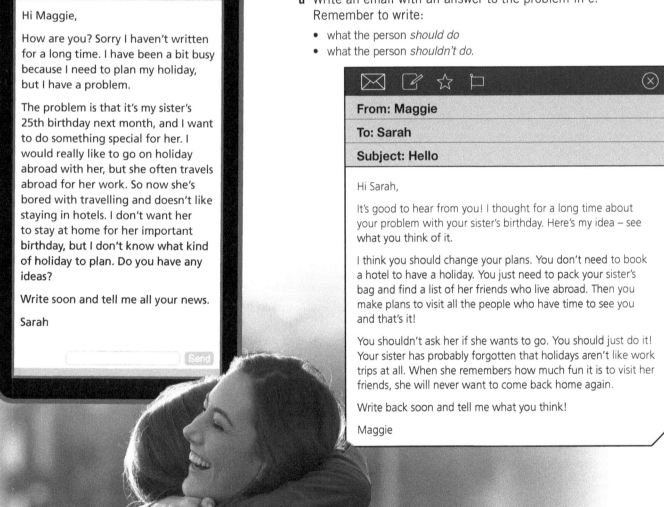

Hi Maggie,

How are you? Sorry I haven't written for a long time. I have been a bit busy because I need to plan my holiday, but I have a problem.

The problem is that it's my sister's 25th birthday next month, and I want to do something special for her. I would really like to go on holiday abroad with her, but she often travels abroad for her work. So now she's bored with travelling and doesn't like staying in hotels. I don't want her to stay at home for her important birthday, but I don't know what kind of holiday to plan. Do you have any ideas?

Write soon and tell me all your news.

Sarah

From: **Maggie**
To: **Sarah**
Subject: **Hello**

Hi Sarah,

It's good to hear from you! I thought for a long time about your problem with your sister's birthday. Here's my idea – see what you think of it.

I think you should change your plans. You don't need to book a hotel to have a holiday. You just need to pack your sister's bag and find a list of her friends who live abroad. Then you make plans to visit all the people who have time to see you and that's it!

You shouldn't ask her if she wants to go. You should just do it! Your sister has probably forgotten that holidays aren't like work trips at all. When she remembers how much fun it is to visit her friends, she will never want to come back home again.

Write back soon and tell me what you think!

Maggie

2 LISTENING

a ▶ **12.06** Listen to the conversation. Complete the sentences.

1 Annette is going to buy an <u>island</u>.
2 Sophie thinks Annette should buy an island with nice b_____.
3 Annette likes the place where her island is because she loves the c_____.
4 From her island, you can see m_____ and w_____.

b ▶ **12.06** Listen to the conversation again and tick (✓) the best endings for the sentences.

1 When Sophie hears that Annette is buying an island, she is …
  a ☐ angry.
  b ✓ surprised.

2 Sophie didn't know that …
  a ☐ people sell islands.
  b ☐ Annette was Emma's friend.

3 Annette is going to stay on the island …
  a ☐ for holidays.
  b ☐ for the whole year.

4 At the moment, there isn't a …
  a ☐ wood on the island.
  b ☐ house on the island.

5 The island that Annette is going to buy …
  a ☐ is warm and sunny.
  b ☐ has lovely views.

6 Annette and her family travel to the island …
  a ☐ in someone else's boat.
  b ☐ in their own boat.

7 Emma is going to …
  a ☐ stay on the island with Annette and her family.
  b ☐ stay on the island when Annette isn't there.

c Write about things you are going to do in the future. Here are some possible ideas:

- live in a different place
- get a different job
- start a new hobby.

Your ideas don't have to be true!

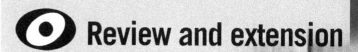

Review and extension

1 GRAMMAR

Correct the sentences.

1 We going to play tennis after school.
  We're going to play tennis after school.
2 Are they go to have a party for David's birthday?
3 I go to go to university next year.
4 I'm going to shopping with my friends on Saturday.
5 Do you going to spend a week in Costa Rica?
6 She not going to study Economics at university.
7 We're going have dinner at a Vietnamese restaurant tonight.
8 Greg going to go skiing in Falls Creek in June. He's so lucky!

2 VOCABULARY

Correct the sentences.

1 In the afternoon, we took the ferry and visited an eyeland.
  In the afternoon, we took the ferry and visited an island.
2 The country side in northeast Turkey is really beautiful.
3 The biggest waterfal in the USA is Niagara Falls.
4 The Sahara is one of the biggest desserts in the world.
5 You can see a lot of beautiful birds in the rain forest.
6 The highest montains in South America are the Andes.
7 There were a lot of sheep in the feild behind the farm.
8 My dog loves swimming in the leik.

3 WORDPOWER *take*

Match 1–6 with a–f to make sentences.

1 [d] It took her
2 ☐ That road is dangerous. Please take
3 ☐ Flying is expensive, so they are going to take
4 ☐ Good morning, sir. Can I take
5 ☐ If you've got a headache, you should take
6 ☐ The bus station? Yes, take

a the train to Kuala Lumpur. It's cheaper.
b the second left, and it's about 500 metres on the right.
c some paracetamol.
d more than an hour to walk to the hotel.
e care when you cross it.
f your bags to your room?

↻ REVIEW YOUR PROGRESS

Look again at Review your progress on p. 128 of the Student's Book. How well can you do these things now?
3 = very well   2 = well   1 = not so well

I CAN …	
talk about holiday plans	☐
give advice	☐
talk about travel	☐
use language for travel and tourism	☐
write an email with travel advice.	☐

VOX POP VIDEO

UNIT 1: People

1a 🎬 Hello, I'm Marie. What's your name?

a Watch video 1a and tick (✓) the correct answers.

1 What does Jenny say?
   a ☐ Hello, I'm Jenny.
   b ☐ Hi, my name's Jenny.
   c ✓ Hi, I'm Jenny.

2 What does Maibritt say?
   a ☐ Hi, my name is Maibritt.
   b ☐ Hello, I'm Maibritt.
   c ☐ Hello, my name's Maibritt.

3 What does Precious say?
   a ☐ I'm called Precious.
   b ☐ I'm Precious.
   c ☐ My name is Precious.

4 What does Dana say?
   a ☐ I'm Dana. Nice to meet you.
   b ☐ Hi, I'm Dana. Good to meet you.
   c ☐ Hey, my name's Dana. Happy to meet you.

5 What does Shelby say?
   a ☐ Hey, my name's Shelby.
   b ☐ Hi, I'm Shelby.
   c ☐ Hello, my name is Shelby.

6 What does Maria say?
   a ☐ Hello, my name is Maria.
   b ☐ Hi, I'm Maria.
   c ☐ Hi, I'm called Maria.

7 What does Lauren say?
   a ☐ Hello, my name's Lauren.
   b ☐ Hi, I'm Lauren.
   c ☐ Good morning. Call me Lauren.

8 What does Matteo say?
   a ☐ Hi, I'm Matteo. Good to meet you.
   b ☐ Hello, my name's Matteo. Pleasure.
   c ☐ Hey, I'm Matteo. Nice to meet you.

1b 🎬 Hi! How are you?

b Watch video 1b. Match the people 1–8 with the sentences a–h.

1	Peter	a	I'm very well, thank you.
2	Malachi	b	I'm good, thanks. And you?
3	Steven	c	I'm fine, thank you.
4	Precious	d	Very well. Enjoying the sun.
5	Andy	e	I'm great today, thanks. You too?
6	Petros	f	Yeah, very well, thanks. Very well.
7	Lauren	g	I'm fine, thank you. Yourself?
8	Christian	h	Very good, thanks. You?

1c 🎬 Where are you from?

c Watch video 1c and underline the correct words to complete the sentences.

1 Maria is from *the USA* / *Argentina* / *Spain*.
2 Matteo is *Spanish* / *American* / *Italian*.
3 Dana is *American* / *British* / *Australian*.
4 Erica is from *Italy* / *Spain* / *Argentina*.
5 Oliviero is from *Milan* / *Rome* / *Venice*.
6 Lauren is from *Great Britain* / *France* / *the USA*.
7 Maria is *Russian* / *Italian* / *French*.

UNIT 2: Work and study

2a 🎬 Are you a student?

a Watch video 2a and tick (✓) the correct answers.

1 Jenny _____.
   a ✓ works
   b ☐ studies

2 Rebecca _____.
   a ☐ studies
   b ☐ works

3 John _____ a student.
   a ☐ is
   b ☐ isn't

4 Suzanne _____.
   a ☐ studies
   b ☐ doesn't study

5 Erica _____.
   a ☐ works
   b ☐ studies

2b 🎬 Do you work full-time or part-time?

b Watch video 2b and underline the correct words to complete the sentences.

1 Rebecca works *part-time* / *full-time*.
2 Jenny is *an administrator* / *a waitress*.
3 John works *part-time* / *full-time*.
4 Erica works *56 hours* / *5 or 6 hours* a week.
5 Suzanne *works* / *doesn't work*.

2c 🎬 What time do you start work?

c Watch video 2c and tick (✓) the correct answers.

1 Today Erica started work at _____.
   a ☐ 10:00
   b ✓ 11:00
   c ☐ 10:30

2 John usually starts work at _____.
   a ☐ 9:30
   b ☐ 8:30
   c ☐ 8:00

3 Suzanne _____ started work at six o'clock in the morning.
  a ☐ always
  b ☐ sometimes
  c ☐ usually

4 Jenny starts work at _____.
  a ☐ 7:30
  b ☐ 8:00
  c ☐ 8:30

UNIT 3: Daily life

3a ■◀ What time do you usually get up?

a Watch video 3a. Complete the sentences with the times in the box.

> 8:30 7:30 ~~7:00~~ 10:00

1 Colin usually gets up at ____*7:00*____.
2 At the weekend, Carolyn usually gets up at _____.
3 Darren usually gets up at _____.
4 Lauren usually gets up at _____.

3b ■◀ What do you do at the weekend?

b Watch video 3b and underline the correct words to complete the sentences.

1 At the weekend Carolyn goes to the *cinema* / *park* / *shopping centre*.
2 At the weekend Colin works in *a shop* / *his office* / *his garden*.
3 At the weekend Darren usually plays *football* / *golf* / *basketball*.
4 At the weekend Lauren goes *shopping* / *to museums* / *to the beach* with her friends.

3c ■◀ What do you think is good about smartphones?

c Watch video 3c and tick (✓) the correct answers.

1 Lauren can read _____ on her smartphone.
  a ☐ the newspaper
  b ✓ books
  c ☐ magazines

2 Darren likes _____ on his smartphone.
  a ☐ listening to music
  b ☐ using the camera
  c ☐ using the satnav

3 Colin thinks the _____ is useful.
  a ☐ camera
  b ☐ satnav
  c ☐ Internet

4 Carolyn likes _____ on her smartphone.
  a ☐ looking at photos
  b ☐ listening to music
  c ☐ watching TV

UNIT 4: Food

4a ■◀ What do you usually have for breakfast?

a Watch video 4a and underline the correct words to complete the sentences.

1 Seb usually has *toast and jam* / *cereal* / *eggs and bacon* for breakfast.
2 Lucy usually has *eggs and bacon* / *toast and jam* / *cereal* for breakfast.
3 Solyman usually has *cereal* / *toast and jam* / *eggs on toast* for breakfast.

4b ■◀ What food do you cook at home?

b Watch video 4b. Complete the sentences with the words in the box.

> curry fish pasta and meat ~~quiche~~

1 Seb sometimes cooks ____*quiche*____.
2 Lucy cooks a lot of _____.
3 Wiktoria cooks _____.
4 Solyman cooks a lot of _____.

4c ■◀ Who do you know who's a good cook?

c Watch video 4c and underline the correct words to complete the sentences.

1 Seb's *brother* / *sister* / *dad* is a very good cook.
2 Seb's *brother and sister* / *mum and dad* / *grandparents* are vegetarians.
3 Lucy's *dad* / *sister* / *best friend* is a very good cook.
4 Lucy's friend *makes fresh soups* / *bakes cakes* / *makes curries*.
5 Solyman's *mum* / *dad* / *brother* is a very good cook.

UNIT 5: Places

5a ▶ What do you like about this city?

a Watch video 5a. Match 1–3 with a–c to make sentences.

1 [c] Precious likes Cambridge because
2 [ ] Christian likes Cambridge because
3 [ ] Adele likes Cambridge because

a it's a beautiful, clean city.
b there's a lot of history and culture.
c it's busy but it's small.

5b ▶ Is there anything you don't like about this city?

b Watch video 5b and <u>underline</u> the correct words to complete the sentences.

1 Precious thinks that Cambridge is *busy* / *small* / *big*.
2 Steven always goes to the same places as *the tourists* / *families* / *the students*.
3 Adele doesn't like the *weather* / *tourists* / *cyclists* in Cambridge.

5c ▶ Can you tell me how to get to Regent Street?

c Watch video 5c and tick (✓) the correct answers.

1 Precious tells Marie how to get to …
   a [ ] Market Square.
   b [ ] Tennis Court Road.
   c [✓] Regent Street.
2 Christian tells Marie how to get to …
   a [ ] Regent Street.
   b [ ] the Regal Cinema.
   c [ ] Market Square.
3 Steven tells Marie how to get to …
   a [ ] Market Square.
   b [ ] the station.
   c [ ] Regent Street.
4 Adele tells Marie how to get to …
   a [ ] Regent Street.
   b [ ] the station.
   c [ ] Market Square.

UNIT 6: Family

6a ▶ Where were your parents born?

a Watch video 6a. Match 1–4 with a–d to make sentences.

1 [b] Mark's father was born in
2 [ ] Laurence's mother was born in
3 [ ] Maibritt's parents were born in
4 [ ] Colin's father was born in

a the Netherlands.
b London.
c Wales.
d Denmark.

6b ▶ Have you got any brothers or sisters?

b Watch video 6b and <u>underline</u> the correct words to complete the sentences.

1 Mark's got *a brother* / *a sister* / *two sisters*.
2 Laurence's got *a brother and a sister* / *a brother* / *a sister*.
3 Colin's got *a younger brother* / *an older sister* / *an older brother*.
4 Maibritt's got *an older sister* / *a younger sister* / *a younger brother*.

6c ▶ What was an important year in your life?

c Watch video 6c and tick (✓) the correct answers.

1 In 2001 Laurence …
   a [ ] got married.
   b [ ] left school.
   c [✓] finished university.
2 In 2003 Maibritt …
   a [ ] left school.
   b [ ] got married.
   c [ ] went to university.
3 In 2005 Colin …
   a [ ] went to university.
   b [ ] got married.
   c [ ] went to the USA.
4 In 1997 Mark …
   a [ ] left school.
   b [ ] got married.
   c [ ] finished university.

UNIT 7: Trips

7a 🎥 How did you travel here today?

a Watch video 7a. Match 1–3 with a–c to make sentences.

1 Laurence travelled   a   by train.
2 Darren travelled   b   by car and by bike.
3 Peter travelled   c   by bike.

7b 🎥 Do you like travelling by plane?

b Watch video 7b and <u>underline</u> the correct words to complete the sentences.

1 Laurence *hates travelling by plane / <u>likes meeting new people</u> / doesn't like going to new places.*
2 Darren *hates travelling by plane / doesn't like airports / doesn't mind travelling by plane.*
3 Peter *hates airports / likes airports / hates travelling by plane.*

7c 🎥 What do you think about the London Underground?

c Watch video 7c and tick (✓) the correct answers.

1 Darren thinks the Underground is …
   a ☐ dirty.
   b ☐ expensive.
   c ☑ amazing.
2 Peter thinks the Underground is …
   a ☐ busy.
   b ☐ expensive.
   c ☐ dirty.
3 The first time Laurence took the Underground he …
   a ☐ lost his ticket.
   b ☐ got lost.
   c ☐ didn't have a map.

UNIT 8: Fit and healthy

8a 🎥 What sports do you watch on TV?

a Watch video 8a and tick (✓) the correct answers.

1 Sammy watches _____ on TV.
   a ☐ football and basketball
   b ☑ tennis and football
   c ☐ football and rugby
2 Stephen watches _____ on TV.
   a ☐ football, cricket and rugby
   b ☐ golf, football and rugby
   c ☐ basketball, football and cricket
3 Babs's favourite sport on TV is _____.
   a ☐ swimming
   b ☐ rugby
   c ☐ golf
4 Malachi loves watching _____ on TV.
   a ☐ football
   b ☐ golf
   c ☐ basketball

8b 🎥 Do you think people have to go to a gym to get fit?

b Watch video 8b and <u>underline</u> the correct words to complete the sentences.

1 Malachi says you *have to / <u>don't have to</u>* go to a gym to get fit.
2 Stephen thinks you can go *swimming / running* to get fit.
3 In Babs's opinion, *swimming / walking* is a good way to get fit.
4 Sammy says that you can go *running / cycling* to get fit.

8c 🎥 What exercise do you do?

c Watch video 8c and tick (✓) the correct answers.

1 Babs goes to a _____ class.
   a ☐ salsa
   b ☐ yoga
   c ☑ keep-fit
2 Sammy plays tennis _____.
   a ☐ every day
   b ☐ once a month
   c ☐ once a week
3 Malachi regularly plays _____.
   a ☐ football
   b ☐ tennis
   c ☐ rugby
4 Stephen sometimes goes _____.
   a ☐ cycling
   b ☐ running
   c ☐ skiing

UNIT 9: Clothes and shopping

9a 🎥 **Where do you usually go shopping for clothes?**

a Watch video 9a and tick (✓) the correct answers.

1 Carolyn _____ going shopping for clothes.
    a ☐ loves
    b ☐ enjoys
    c ✓ doesn't enjoy

2 Mark normally goes to _____.
    a ☐ shopping malls
    b ☐ department stores
    c ☐ fashionable boutiques

3 Matt goes shopping for clothes in _____.
    a ☐ shopping malls
    b ☐ department stores
    c ☐ the high street

4 Lauren sometimes goes shopping for clothes in _____.
    a ☐ London
    b ☐ Oxford
    c ☐ shopping malls

9b 🎥 **Do you ever ask friends or family to help you buy clothes?**

b Watch video 9b and underline the correct words to complete the sentences.

1 Carolyn usually goes shopping *with her boyfriend* / *alone* / *with friends*.
2 Mark *sometimes* / *never* / *always* asks friends or family to help him buy clothes.
3 Matt *usually* / *always* / *never* chooses his clothes.
4 Lauren prefers to go shopping for clothes *with friends* / *alone* / *with her mother*.

9c 🎥 **Can you describe the clothes that you are wearing now?**

c Watch video 9c. Complete the sentences with the words from the box.

| black shoes blue trousers ~~blue jeans~~ |
| a black and white dress |

1 Carolyn is wearing _blue jeans_.
2 Matt is wearing _____.
3 Lauren is wearing _____.
4 Mark is wearing _____.

UNIT 10: Communication

10a 🎥 **How do you usually contact your friends?**

a Watch video 10a and underline the correct words to complete the sentences.

1 Mitchell *never* / *often* / *always* uses Facebook to contact his friends.
2 Andy *never* / *often* / *usually* phones his friends.
3 Shelby *always* / *usually* / *never* texts her friends.
4 William *sometimes* / *never* / *always* contacts his friends on Facebook.

10b 🎥 **Which is better for you, a laptop or a tablet?**

b Watch video 10b. Match 1–4 with a–d to make sentences.

1 ☐ c Andy prefers to use a laptop because
2 ☐ Shelby prefers a tablet because
3 ☐ Mitchell would like a tablet because
4 ☐ William's laptop is very useful because

a it's easier to move around.
b he can use it for work.
c the screen is bigger.
d it's a lot more useful.

10c 🎥 **Which languages can you speak?**

c Watch video 10c and tick (✓) the correct answers.

1 William can speak …
    a ☐ French and Italian.
    b ✓ French and German.
    c ☐ Italian and Spanish.

2 Mitchell can speak …
    a ☐ English and French.
    b ☐ French and German.
    c ☐ English and German.

3 Shelby can speak …
    a ☐ French and English.
    b ☐ English and German.
    c ☐ Spanish and English.

UNIT 11: Entertainment

11a ▶️ Have you read any Harry Potter books?

a Watch video 11a and <u>underline</u> the correct words to complete the sentences.

1 Petros *has read some* / *hasn't read any* Harry Potter books.
2 Dee Dee *has seen most* / *hasn't seen any* of the Harry Potter films.
3 James *hasn't read* / *has read all* the Harry Potter books.
4 Ayden *doesn't like* / *really likes* the Harry Potter films.

11b ▶️ Have you seen a film with good special effects?

b Watch video 11b and tick (✓) the correct answers.

1 Petros _____ the special effects in *Avatar* very much.
   a ✓ liked
   b ☐ didn't like

2 In Dee Dee's opinion, the special effects in *Transformers* _____ very good.
   a ☐ are
   b ☐ aren't

3 Ayden thinks the special effects in *The Matrix* _____ very good.
   a ☐ weren't
   b ☐ were

11c ▶️ Which kinds of music do you often listen to?

c Watch video 11c. Complete the sentences with the words in the box.

all kinds of   American pop   ~~acoustic~~   old R & B

1 Petros really enjoys listening to *acoustic* music.
2 Dee Dee enjoys listening to _____ music.
3 James enjoys listening to _____ music.
4 Ayden secretly enjoys listening to _____ music.

UNIT 12: Travel

12a ▶️ Are you going to go on holiday this summer?

a Watch video 12a and <u>underline</u> the correct words to complete the sentences.

1 Lauren is going to Paris for *five days* / *one week* / *two weeks*.
2 Patrick is going to Italy *at the beginning* / *in the middle* / *at the end* of August.
3 Oliviero is going to Greece *tomorrow* / *next week* / *next month*.
4 Adam is going to Dubai in *September* / *November* / *December*.
5 Dana is going to Dublin for *five days* / *seven days* / *ten days*.

12b ▶️ What one thing should you always take on holiday?

b Watch video 12b. Match 1–6 with a–f to make sentences.

1 ☐d In Matteo's opinion, when you go on holiday you should always take
2 ☐ In Lauren's opinion, when you go on holiday you should always take
3 ☐ In Patrick's opinion, when you go on holiday you should always take
4 ☐ In Oliviero's opinion, when you go on holiday you should always take
5 ☐ In Dana's opinion, when you go on holiday you should always take
6 ☐ In Adam's opinion, when you go on holiday you should always take

a a phone to take pictures.
b your passport.
c something children will like.
d a good guidebook.
e good company.
f a camera.

12c ▶️ Where do you think visitors to England should go?

c Watch video 12c and tick (✓) the correct answers.

1 Lauren _____ to England before.
   a ☐ has been
   b ✓ hasn't been

2 Oliviero has visited _____.
   a ☐ Cambridge and London
   b ☐ London and Oxford

3 _____ is one of Adam's favourite places in England.
   a ☐ Cambridge
   b ☐ The Lake District

4 Patrick thinks that visitors should go to the _____ of England.
   a ☐ north
   b ☐ south

5 Dana thinks that visitors should visit _____.
   a ☐ the Tower of London
   b ☐ Big Ben

AUDIOSCRIPTS

Unit 1

▶ 01.01

Turkish	American
Iranian	Russian
Irish	Mexican
Japanese	Nigerian
Saudi	Colombian

▶ 01.02

1 I like Beatriz. She's a warm and friendly person.
2 Our new teacher's really cool and he's very popular with his students.
3 Taylor Swift's a very well-known singer. Her new song's fantastic!
4 My friend Dani's a lovely person. She's really kind to all her friends.
5 Dusit is very quiet, but he's a great friend.
6 Mr Jones is a very pleasant person and he's a brilliant teacher.

▶ 01.03

chat	quiz
cake	capital
keep	bike
know	chart

▶ 01.04

1 How can I help?
2 I'd like to do a fitness class.
3 What's your surname?
4 Sorry – can you spell that, please?
5 What time's the next class?
6 It's tomorrow at half past six. / It's at half past six tomorrow.
7 Where's the class?
8 It's in Studio 3.
9 So that's 6:30 in Studio 3?
10 Thanks for your help.
11 You're welcome.

▶ 01.05

A Hello. How can I help?
B Hi. I'd like to do a German class. I'm a beginner.
A No problem.
B When are the classes?
A They're on Mondays at 7:30.
B Great. Can I book a place on the course?
A Certainly. What's your surname?
B Cumberbatch.
A Sorry – can you spell that, please?
B C-U-M-B-E-R-B-A-T-C-H.
A Thank you. Enjoy the class.

▶ 01.06

1	Certainly.	7	Of course.
2	Good idea.	8	Is he from London?
3	Sorry?	9	Yes, he is.
4	Me?	10	Is she Italian?
5	Sure.	11	No, she isn't.
6	Off to the gym?	12	No problem.

▶ 01.07

1	three	6	match
2	eight	7	brother
3	twelve	8	warm
4	sixteen	9	kitchen
5	right	10	well-known

▶ 01.08

KEREM You're new at this football club, aren't you?
PEDRO Yes. My name's Pedro.
K Hi, Pedro, I'm Kerem. Welcome to the club. Where are you from?
P I'm from Segovia, in Spain.
K Really? My grandma's Spanish. She's from Cádiz.
P Do you speak Spanish?
K Yes, but not very well.
P Maybe we can speak Spanish together sometimes?

K OK. I'd like to do that. I think Spanish is *really* difficult.
P It isn't for me!
K Ha ha! No, of course it isn't! Do you want to play with the club every week?
P Yes. I love football.
K Me too.
P Where's the match next week?
K It's in Bolu.
P Is that far away?
K No, it isn't far, but you need to drive there.
P Oh dear. I don't have a car.
K Don't worry. You can come with us.
P Thanks! That's really kind.
K No problem. Be ready by nine o'clock.
P Great. See you next week!

Unit 2

▶ 02.01

1 She works as a receptionist in a big hotel.
2 He's a Russian businessman.
3 My father's an engineer.
4 Jack works as a mechanic for Mercedes.
5 My uncle's a taxi driver in London.
6 Brad Pitt's a well-known American actor.
7 My secretary speaks excellent English.
8 She works as a tour guide in Rome.
9 He's a very friendly police officer.
10 Where's the photographer?

▶ 02.02

watches	finishes
likes	plays
goes	teaches
stops	works
uses	freezes

▶ 02.03

1 A Can I have a coffee, please?
  B Of course. White or black?
2 A I'd like some help with my homework, please.
  B Sorry, not now. I'm busy.
  A That's OK. It doesn't matter.
3 A Could you pass me my phone, please?
  B Sure, no problem. Here you are.
4 A Could we meet tomorrow morning?
  B I'm really sorry. I'm not free.
  A Oh, well, that's a pity.

▶ 02.04

pound	fought
journey	our
tour	flavour

▶ 02.05

ALEX Hi, Dan!
DAN Hi! It's great to see you, Alex. How's school this year?
A Not good. It's really hard work! We have important exams at the end of term. I have so much homework every day, and my dad still wants me to help in his shop. He doesn't understand how important it is to get good marks.
D You're lucky! My dad *only* wants me to study! He wants me to be a pilot like him.
A And do you want to be a pilot?
D No! I know it's not possible because I'm so bad at maths. I always fail my maths exams, and you have to pass them to be a pilot.
A What *do* you want to do?
D I want to be a photographer. I want to take photos of famous people and travel all over the world.
A What does your dad think about that?
D He thinks it's a stupid idea. He won't pay for my studies if I do that, only if I study to become a pilot.
A Well, pilots travel all over the world, too.
D That's just what my dad says!

Unit 3

▶ 03.01

1 I go to the gym twice a week.
2 How often does your brother play football?
3 Caroline eats fruit every day.
4 Do they often go to the Chinese restaurant?
5 We go on holiday three times a year.
6 My brother never does any exercise.

▶ 03.02

computer	laptop
headphones	camera
tablet	printer
smartwatch	speaker
keyboard	smartphone

▶ 03.03

CHRIS Why don't we play tennis this weekend?
LUCY Tennis? Yeah, that'd be great!
C How about on Sunday afternoon?
L Mm, perhaps. Let me see. Oh, I'm sorry, I can't. I usually visit my grandmother on Sundays.
C Are you free on Saturday, then?
L Yes, Saturday's fine.
C Great. Why don't you ask Tanya, too?
L Yes, that's a lovely idea.

▶ 03.04

TOM Why don't we try that new Japanese restaurant this weekend?
LUKE Yes, I'd love to. The question is when?
T How about on Friday?
L Mm, perhaps. Let me see. No, I'm sorry, I can't.
T Oh, that's a pity. Why not?
L I need to work late on Friday.
T OK, no problem. Are you free on Saturday?
L Yes, I am. Saturday's fine.
T Why don't you bring your sister, too?
L Sure. That's a really good idea.
T Great. See you on Saturday.

▶ 03.05

1 Why don't we go to the cinema?
2 Yes, Monday's fine.
3 Do you want to have a coffee after the lesson?
4 Can I bring Leo?
5 Here's your coffee, Annie.
6 Yes, I'd love to.
7 That'd be great.
8 Why don't we try it?

▶ 03.06

MATEO Hi, Clara. How are you?
CLARA Hello, Mateo. Fine, thanks. How are you?
M Great, thanks.
C Good. By the way, it's my birthday next Saturday. Would you like to join us for dinner at my house?
M Yes, I'd love to. It would be great to see you, Gabriel and Sergio again.
C Oh, good! And it's my graduation party on the 18th. Would you like to come to that, too?
M I'd love to, but I'm afraid I can't. I've got an important business trip to Bilbao that weekend and I can't change it.
C Never mind. It doesn't matter.
M I hope you all have a great time at the graduation party. See you on Saturday.
C Yeah, I'm really looking forward to it. Bye!

▶ 03.07

LENA Look, Adam – I've got a new smart speaker. It's great. It does everything for me. Have you got one?
ADAM No, I haven't got anything like that. Not even a tablet.
L Really? Why not?
A I don't want to own a lot of gadgets.

L But they're so useful! How do you get the latest news? And what about music? My smart speaker sounds amazing. I use it all the time.

A Well, I've got a laptop, so I read the news on that. But I've only got it because I need it for my studies.

L I think you need a smart speaker, too! Why don't we have coffee next week and we can look for one online? Bring your laptop.

A OK, that'd be great. How about Monday, after our lesson?

L Sure. Where should we meet?

A How about the Tin Cup Café? It's on Bridge Street. Do you know where that is?

L No, but I can use the map on my smartphone! That's another reason gadgets are so useful!

A OK, OK, I can see that gadgets are useful. And I'd love to meet you for coffee, anyway!

Unit 4

▶ 04.01

see	parent	meet
hair	say	hate
meat	bear	air
pair	need	play
great	date	sheep

▶ 04.02

1 Would you like roasted potatoes or boiled potatoes?
  I'd like boiled potatoes, please.
2 Would you like fried fish or grilled fish?
  I'd like grilled fish, please.
3 Would you like roasted vegetables or grilled vegetables?
  I'd like roasted vegetables, please.
4 Would you like a fried egg or a boiled egg?
  I'd like a fried egg, please.
5 Would you like a can of cola or a bottle of cola?
  I'd like a bottle of cola, please.
6 Would you like a can of soup or a packet of soup?
  I'd like a can of soup, please.
7 Would you like a tin of tomatoes or fresh tomatoes?
  I'd like a tin of tomatoes, please.
8 Would you like a packet of crisps or a bar of chocolate?
  I'd like a packet of crisps, please.

▶ 04.03

WAITRESS Good evening. Do you have a reservation?
PAUL Yes, we have a reservation for six people.
W Certainly. What's the name?
P Henderson.
W Yes, that's fine.
P Can we have a table outside, please?
W Yes, of course. This way, please. Those two over there are both free.
P What do you think? The one on the right?
JENNY I'm not sure. What about the one on the left?
P If you prefer. It's your birthday.
J Well, maybe not. This one's fine.

▶ 04.04

A Are you ready to order?
B Yes, I think so.
A What would you like for your starter?
B I'd like the mixed bean salad, please.
A And for your main course?
B I'll have the chicken curry.
A Would you like chips with that?
B Yes, please.
A And for your starter, madam?
C I'll have the fried fish, please.
A Fried fish in lemon sauce.
C Then I'd like the steak. No, wait. I'll have the spaghetti.
B Oh, that's a good idea. Can I change my order?
A Yes, of course.
B I'll have the same. Spaghetti with meatballs for my main.

▶ 04.05

1 I'd like the chicken salad and then the steak.
2 Can we have a table for four by the window if possible?
3 Where would you like to sit – inside or outside?

4 Would you like to order now or do you need some more time?
5 I'll have the soup, and the spaghetti for my main.
6 I'd like the lamb curry with some rice.

▶ 04.06

1 I'd like the chicken curry, please.
2 Can we have a table by the window if possible?
3 I'd like the mushroom soup for my starter.
4 Would you like to order now?
5 I'll have the spaghetti for my main.
6 Where would you like to sit – outside?

▶ 04.07

EVIE Look at the snow! We can't get out of the house!
ETHAN Oh no! We can't get to the supermarket. What can we eat?
EV Oh, Ethan, you always think about food!
ET But we *need* food. What do we have?
EV Let's look in the kitchen.
ET There isn't much food here.
EV Yes, there is. Look, here's some bread.
ET And is there jam to go on it?
EV No …
ET What about burgers?
EV No, there aren't any burgers in the fridge.
ET Crisps?
EV No …
ET Yoghurt?
EV No …
ET Well, what can we eat? I'm *hungry.*
EV Don't worry, Ethan, we have lots of things. Look … chocolate, onions, bread ….
ET But they don't make a meal.
EV It's OK. I can make a meal with them.
ET Really?
EV Sure. You wait!
…
EV Ta-dah! Here's your starter.
ET What's this?
EV Rice and cheese soup.
ET Oh, Evie! That's terrible!
EV No, it's not! Try some.
ET OK, just a little. Mmmm. You're right – it's good. What's for main course?
EV Fried onions with carrot sandwiches.
ET I don't believe it! Hmm, I'm not so sure about this dish! There isn't a dessert, is there?
EV Of course there is – boiled pasta with chocolate sauce!

Unit 5

▶ 05.01

| 1 | bit | 3 | pie | 5 | part |
| 2 | put | 4 | bear | 6 | pea |

▶ 05.02

box	door
furniture	sink
hard	armchair
lamp	president
curtains	wardrobe
test	mad

▶ 05.03

A Excuse me. Can you tell me the way to the Grand Hotel, please?
B Yes, of course. Go straight on for about 200 metres, then turn left into Broad Street.
A So, straight on, then turn left into Broad Street?
B Yes, that's right. Then go straight along Broad Street until you come to the Regal Cinema and turn right into King's Avenue.
A So, that's right into King's Avenue after the cinema?
B Yes, then go along King's Avenue for about 100 metres. The hotel is on your left.
A Great. Thanks very much.

▶ 05.04

1 Go straight on until you come to a metro station on your left.
2 Turn left at the cinema and go along Huntingdon Road for 250 metres.
3 Can you tell us how to get to the station, please?
4 Go along the High Street for 100 metres, and the concert hall is on your right.
5 Is there a bus stop near here?

6 So, straight on for 250 metres, then turn right into Park Street?
7 That's right. It's on the corner next to the bank.
8 Excuse me. How do I get to the train station from here?

▶ 05.05

1 Go along Acacia Road.
2 Go straight on until you come to the hospital.
3 Can you tell me how to get to the swimming pool, please?
4 Go straight on for about 200 metres.
5 Turn right into Carlisle Avenue.
6 The sports centre is on the left.
7 Is there a bank near here?
8 Go straight on for about 200 metres.

▶ 05.06

JACK Dom, hi – it's Jack here. I'm outside the restaurant, but I can't see you.
DOM That's strange. I'm outside the restaurant, but I can't see *you*.
J What's the name of the restaurant?
D The Panorama.
J Well, that explains it! I'm outside the Flame & Grill. Don't worry – if you're in the square, you're very close. Just look for the post office and turn right. Go down that road, and the Flame & Grill restaurant is on your left.
D OK, see you in a minute or two.
D Jack, it's Dom again. I'm at the post office, but you can't turn right here – there isn't a road!
J What? Don't tell me you're at the wrong post office, too? OK, what else can you see?
D Well, I'm right next to the bridge, so I can see the river. And there's a theatre on my right.
J A theatre? There's no theatre near here.
D But I don't understand. I have your email here, and it says, 'Start at Adenauerplatz metro station and go straight ahead'. I must be somewhere near you.
J Adenauerplatz? No, Dom, read it again. It doesn't say Adenauerplatz. It says Alexanderplatz.
D Oh, no! That explains everything!

Unit 6

▶ 06.01

1 My mother was a terrible student.
2 **A:** Was he at work today?
  B: No, he wasn't.
3 Were you at the party?
4 We were good friends.
5 Peter was an engineer.
6 **A:** Was he married?
  B: Yes, he was.

▶ 06.02

1	nineteen sixty-eight	4	two thousand and six
2	twenty fifteen	5	twenty fourteen
3	nineteen thirty-nine	6	fourteen ninety-two

▶ 06.03

1	closed	6	studied
2	waited	7	visited
3	decided	8	opened
4	arrived	9	started
5	loved	10	worked

▶ 06.04

CONVERSATION 1
IAN Hello, this is Ian Smith. I'm not here right now. Please leave a message after the tone.
ABBY Hi, Ian. Can you call me back? You can call me on my work number or on my mobile.
CONVERSATION 2
DAVID Hello. Ian's phone.
A Oh, hello. Is Ian there, please?
D Sorry, he isn't here just now. He's in a meeting.
A That's OK. It's his sister, Abby. Can he call me back?
D OK, I'll tell him. He'll be back soon. Oh, just a minute. Here he comes now … Ian, it's Abby.
I Hi, Abby. It's me.
A Hello, Ian. At last!

▶ 06.05

1 Please leave a message after the tone.
2 Can you call me back this afternoon?
3 Can you wait a minute?

83

4   You can call me on my home phone or my mobile.
5   I'm not here right now.
6   Sorry, she isn't here just now.

fall	language	manage
date	draw	email
cottage	happy	ball
am	walk	man
cake	Saturday	name

▶ 06.07

MARIA My aunt and uncle have got ten children. So that's ten cousins, and they're all girls.
JAMES Ten? That's amazing! How old are they?
M Well, that's a good question! Mollie's two. She's the baby of the family. And Tara is 25, and has two children of her own. In fact, her daughter Lexie is three now and Mollie is two!
J So … Lexie has an aunt who's younger than her?
M That's right. It's strange, isn't it?
J Why did your aunt and uncle have so many children?
M They just love kids! They say they decided to have three, but when they had three, they wanted another … and another … and another! They bought a really big house, and had more and more children!
J And are you friends with them all?
M Yes, especially the ones that are around the same age as me. When I was a kid, I spent a lot of time with them. We lived near them, so I saw them a lot and they often came to our house. We all played football together, and we often took picnics and went off into the countryside. We had a lot of fun.
J It must be a lot of work for your aunt and uncle.
M It is. But my grandparents help them and my cousins do a lot of jobs in the house – much more than I do!
J So how many brothers and sisters do you have?
M None! My aunt and uncle already had four children when I was born, and my dad – who is my aunt's brother – says he looked at them and decided that one child was enough for him. I think my grandparents were pleased about that!

▶ 06.08

MIA Hi, Bella. How was your weekend?
BELLA Oh, hello, Mia. It was really good, thanks. On Saturday night I went out to a restaurant with Luca.
M Really? Where?
B We went to the new Vietnamese restaurant in the city centre. It was really good.
M But isn't it far from your flat?
B Yes, it is, so we went there by bus. And we went home by taxi.
M Lucky you! Do you want to go for a walk?
B No, I'm sorry, I can't. I need to go shopping. We haven't got anything for dinner.
M OK, never mind. See you soon!

Unit 7

▶ 07.01

thought
south
how
ball
now
law
bought
mouth
daughter
house

▶ 07.02

1   comfortable
2   dangerous
3   uncomfortable
4   expensive

▶ 07.03

1   **A** Excuse me, but I think that's my suitcase.
    B Is it? I'm so sorry. I took the wrong one.
    A That's OK. They look the same.

2   **A** I'm so sorry I didn't come to your party.
    B It doesn't matter. Are you OK?
    A I'm all right now, but I didn't feel well yesterday.
3   **A** Excuse me, please Can you explain that again, please?
    B No problem. German grammar is very hard.

▶ 07.04

1   I'm very sorry I'm late. I didn't hear my alarm.
2   I'm sorry I lost your keys. I always lose things.
3   I'm so sorry I broke your phone. It fell into the bath.
4   I'm sorry I hit your car. The road was very wet.
5   I'm really sorry I didn't reply to your message. Work was very busy today.

▶ 07.05

1   He's very tired today.
2   I'm so sorry I'm late.
3   We're really busy at the moment.
4   It's very cold outside.
5   I'm really sorry I can't come.
6   We're so lost!

▶ 07.06

LARA What did you do in the summer holidays last year?
RICK I went to France. I took my bike over on the ferry from England.
L That's funny – I went to France, too! But I caught an aeroplane from London to Nice.
R I hate travelling in aeroplanes because I'm so tall. There's never enough space for my legs, so it's always really uncomfortable.
L Oh, I went first class, so it wasn't a problem. Where did you go on your bike?
R I took a train to the Loire valley, and after that I cycled everywhere.
L That sounds like hard work!
R Not to me – I love riding my bike through the countryside. You see so much that way. What about you? What's Nice like?
L Oh, it's lovely, with the beach in front and the hills behind. And I stayed in a fantastic hotel. It was an old castle, and the rooms were beautiful and so comfortable!
R I didn't stay in hotels. I don't have enough money. I used a website where you can stay in people's homes. It's a cheap way to travel, and you meet lots of interesting people.
L It sounds horrible. I hate staying with people I don't know. And I don't think it's very safe.
R I didn't have any problems. I love meeting people, and I learned so much about France. I often ate dinner with them, too, so I tried lots of food I don't have at home. That was really interesting.
L I like to choose what I eat. There are so many fantastic restaurants in Nice. I was there for three weeks, so I went to most of them!
R Wasn't that very expensive?
L Oh, probably. I didn't really think about it. I just used my credit card. My parents pay the bill.
R Wow! Do they pay for everything?
L Yes, they do, which is lucky, because I love shopping. And there are lots of great shops in Nice. In fact, I love it so much that on my last day I went shopping and forgot about the time. I missed my plane!
R Oh, dear! At least that's one problem I'm sure I'll never have!

Unit 8

▶ 08.01

a   Can you speak French?
b   Yes, I can.
c   I can't ski very well.
d   Can he play the piano?
e   No, he can't.
f   We can take the train to Manchester.
g   She can't play tennis very well.
h   He can't run that fast.

▶ 08.02

1   **A** What's the matter?
    B Nothing. I've just got a bit of a stomach ache.
2   **A** How do you feel?
    B Well, actually, I feel really awful.
3   **A** Are you all right?
    B Yes, I'm fine now, thanks.
4   **A** Does your knee hurt?
    B Yes, it does. It hurts when I walk.
5   **A** Have you got a temperature?
    B No, I haven't. I just feel a bit tired.

▶ 08.03

TONY Hi, Judy. Good to see you. How are you?
JUDY Er, I'm not sure.
T Hey, Judy. Are you all right?
J Well, actually, I don't feel very well.
T You don't look very well.
J I think I've got a temperature.
T Do you feel sick?
J Yes, a bit, and I've got an awful headache.
T You poor thing! Come and sit down. I'll get you a glass of water.
J OK, thanks.

▶ 08.04

1   That man over there doesn't dance very well.
2   My uncle has got two big dogs.
3   Thank you very much, madam. Have a good day.
4   We've got a really big garden at our house.
5   There's a small lake in the middle of the park.

▶ 08.05

ROSA Hi, Emilia.
EMILIA Hi, Rosa. Are you OK? You don't look well.
R No, my back hurts. I'm sorry, but I can't play badminton with you today.
E That's OK. What happened?
R I was ice skating with my sister, and I fell flat on my back. The pain was terrible! I couldn't walk at all for a few days.
E Oh, I'm so sorry to hear that!
R Can you play badminton with someone else today?
E Yes, no problem. I'll ask Lana. I don't have to be at my next lecture until two. Would you like to go for a coffee?
R Yes, that would be great.
R I'm a bit worried about my back. My dad has a bad back, and he has a lot of problems with it. I don't want to be like that.
E Well, my mum has the same problem. She does yoga now, and she says that it really helps.
R Really? That's great, but yoga seems so difficult. And I would feel nervous doing yoga in front of strangers.
E There are a lot of different levels of yoga classes. My mum was in a beginner's class when she first started. She told me that everyone is really friendly, and the yoga teachers are always very helpful. But you don't have to go to a class. There are a lot of good yoga classes online.
R That's a great idea, Emilia. Would you like to try an online yoga class with me?
E Yeah, sure! I need to do something like that. I can't even touch my toes. Can you?
R Well, I could before my skating accident. The doctor says I should be careful, so maybe I should go to a class where a teacher can help me in person, and not online.
E OK. Do you want to go to a class tomorrow evening?
R I can't tomorrow. I have a piano lesson, but what about Thursday evening?

Unit 9

▶ 09.01

1   **A** What are you doing here?
    B I'm waiting for my brother.
2   **A** Where's Michael going?
    B He's looking for his brother.
3   **A** Are you having your dinner now?
    B Yes, we are. We're having spaghetti bolognese.
4   **A** What are you buying?
    B I'm not buying anything. I'm just looking.
5   **A** It isn't raining at the moment.
    B In fact, the sun's shining now.

▶ 09.02

1 This is one of the biggest shopping centres in the world.
2 There are over two hundred and fifty clothes shops.
3 There are about twenty-three bookshops.
4 If you can't find a shop, you can ask someone at the information desk for help.
5 It can be hard to find a space in the car park.
6 I waited for over an hour at the bus stop.

▶ 09.03

EMMA Hi, Joe. What are you buying?
JOE Hello, Emma. I'm buying some new trousers.
E But you usually wear jeans and trainers.
J Yes, I know. I'm trying to dress smartly in my new job.
E Well, I like them.
J Good, and, look, I'm wearing some new shoes that I bought yesterday.
E Wow, they look great!
J Thanks. Are you wearing a new dress?
E Yes, I am. What do you think?
J It's really nice. Hey, do you want to go for a coffee?
E Sorry, I can't. I'm waiting for my boyfriend. He's parking the car.
J OK, never mind. Bye!

▶ 09.04

vote	boat
some	brother
soup	cool
dollar	on
rock	cough
pool	do
other	love
toe	hope

▶ 09.05

1 **A** Can I help you?
  B Yes, I'm looking for a red dress and some smart shoes.
2 **A** Can I try them on?
  B Certainly. The fitting rooms are over there.
3 **A** What size are you?
  B 32, I think.
4 **A** What colour would you like?
  B Blue or green, please.
5 **A** What do you think?
  B It looks really good on you.
6 **A** How much are these jeans, please?
  B They're £49.99.

▶ 09.06

1 I'm a size 10.
2 It looks good on you.
3 How much is it?
4 The jeans are over there.

▶ 09.07

PART 1

BOY Oh no! Can you see what Dad's wearing?
GIRL Not the jumper that Grandma made him?
B That's right. The one with an elephant on the front.
G For the *party*? On Mum's *birthday*? How could he do this to her? Oh, *why* doesn't she say something? Can't she make him wear something else? Look, she's talking to him now. Perhaps she's asking him to take it off before the visitors arrive.
B No, I don't think so. I think they're just talking about the drinks. Yes, they're getting more glasses from the kitchen.
G But that jumper's terrible! Especially for a party. Can't he see how lovely Mum looks in her beautiful dress and her jewellery? I love that gold necklace she's wearing.
B I know.

PART 2

ANDREW Oh, hello, Mother.
GRANDMOTHER Hello, Andrew. I came a bit early so I could help you and Sarah with the food.
A That's very kind. Sarah's in the kitchen, making sandwiches. I'm sure she'd love you to help.

GR Oh look! You're wearing the jumper I made! How nice!
A Yes, of course I am. It's my favourite, and it's a special party tonight.
GR Ah, Andrew. What a lovely son you are!
B OK, now I understand. He did it to please Grandma.
GI Yes, but he still looks stupid.

PART 3

A Well, the first visitors are here. The party's started!
GR How exciting!
A Do you know, Mother, I'm so excited that I'm getting quite hot.
GR Oh dear, yes. That jumper's a bit warm for a party, isn't it?
A I think it is. Ah well, I can put it on again tomorrow.
GR Of course you can.
B Look, he's wearing his best shirt under it!
GI That was his plan all the time, wasn't it?
B Clever Dad! He made Grandma happy *and* he looks good for the party.

Unit 10

▶ 10.01

1 seven thousand five hundred
2 eight hundred and twelve
3 two million five hundred thousand
4 one thousand, two hundred and ninety-nine
5 two thousand and one

▶ 10.02

1 English is the most popular language in the world.
2 The Gambia is one of the smallest countries in Africa.
3 This is one of the most dangerous cities in the world.
4 Brazil is the biggest country in Latin America.
5 Spanish is one of the most useful languages in the world.
6 This is the most expensive restaurant in the city.
7 This is one of the saddest films ever.
8 This is the heaviest thing in my bag.

▶ 10.03

A Could you help me with something?
B Yes, of course. What is it?
A I don't know how to record programmes on my new TV.
B Right, that's easy.
A Would you mind showing me?
B No, not at all. So, what you do is this. First, you go to the programme menu, then you find the programme you want and, finally, you press 'Record'.
A OK, that looks easy. Now let me try. So first I go to the programme menu?
B Yes, that's right.
A Then I find the programme I want with these arrows, like this?
B Correct.
A And then I just press the 'Record' button. Is that right?
B Yes, perfect. Well done!

▶ 10.04

1 **A** Could you help me with my homework?
  B Yes, of course.
2 Can you explain that to me?
3 **A** Would you mind helping me?
  B No, not at all.
4 **A** Do you mind showing me how to take photos with my phone?
  B No problem.
5 So first I click on this link?
6 Next, I put in my password, like this?
7 And then I press this button. Is that right?

▶ 10.05

1 Can you help me with something?
2 Would you mind showing me how to do it?
3 Could you explain that again, please?
4 Do you mind helping me with my shopping?

▶ 10.06

1 How do I check my email?
2 Can you show me how to log in?
3 What's the problem with your computer?
4 Would you mind speaking more slowly, please?
5 Do you mind showing me how to take photos?
6 How often do you check your email?

▶ 10.07

Hello! You are listening to *Side Salad*. Today, I want to talk about growing old. There are now more Americans over 100 years old. In 2019, there were about 80,000 people over 100. And in 2014, there were 72,197 Americans 100 years old or older. Just because Americans are living longer now, does it mean they are healthy?

In Loma Linda, California, there is a 'Blue Zone'. Blue Zones are places that have the highest number of people 100 years old or older. The people who live in Loma Linda don't smoke, eat sugar, dance or watch TV. They also eat a lot of fruit, nuts and vegetables. They eat very little meat. The people here are very close to one another. In another Blue Zone located in Costa Rica, people eat mostly beans and corn tortillas. They also move into old age and feel good about life. A third Blue Zone located in Okinawa is the home to the world's oldest women. They also do exercises and eat a lot of vegetables.

So what things do these places share, and why do the people there live to be 100 years old? Scientists think it is because they all do some form of exercise, eat a lot of vegetables and are close to their friends, families and neighbours. In other words, they are happier!

But don't worry. If you don't live in a Blue Zone, there are many other things you can do to live your happiest and best life. First, try to sleep 7 to 8 hours every night for a longer life. Right now, 1 in 3 adults are not getting enough sleep, and this causes many illnesses. Second, drink coffee or tea. Both coffee and tea drinkers are in 20 to 30% less danger of early death. Third, keep a healthy social network. This can help you live up to 50% longer. In fact, having 3 close friends in your social network may lower the danger of early death by 200%. So, go out and meet a friend at your favourite coffee shop. And remember, keep smiling!

Unit 11

▶ 11.01

1 I've never read any novels by Ernest Hemingway.
2 Have you ever stayed in that hotel?
3 He's driven to Paris six times this year.
4 Ella and Greg have never met you.
5 Have you ever bought a new car?
6 She hasn't met the president before.

▶ 11.02

1 He's a brilliant actor.
2 She's a famous Hollywood film director.
3 I went to the theatre in London last night.
4 She was a well-known model when she was young.
5 I'd like to be a fashion photographer.
6 She's won several national prizes.
7 He's the best musician in our family.
8 The orchestra played for three hours.

▶ 11.03

TIM So what did you think of the film?
SAM I really liked the film. How about you?
T I thought it was quite good, but it was a bit long.
S Yeah, maybe.
T Did you like the music?
S Yes, I thought it was great.
T Did you? I thought it was a bit loud. Sometimes I couldn't hear the actors very well.
S Really? I thought the music was fine. Also, I thought the photography was great.
T Yes, me too. But I didn't like the actor who was Nelson Mandela.
S No, me neither. Anyway, let's go for a coffee.

▶ 11.04

1 **A** I thought the film was brilliant.
  B Did you?

2 **A** I really liked the music.
  B Me too.
3 **A** I love going to the theatre.
  B Do you?
4 **A** I didn't like Tom Cruise's last film.
  B Me neither.

▶ 11.05

MARIANNE So, Lenny, what's the most interesting place you've been to?
LENNY Well, Marianne, I've been to lots of great places, but I think Mexico was probably the most interesting. I loved learning about the history, and I've never seen such beautiful beaches before! Also, the food is fantastic.
M What's it like? I've never tried Mexican food.
L Lots of meat! Lots of beans. And fantastic fruit.
M Hmm. I don't eat meat, so I'm not sure it would be so good for me.
L So how about you? Where's your favourite place?
M Probably Italy. I've been there a few times, and I always enjoy it. I have a friend in the city of Bologna, which has some of the best restaurants in Italy. I think I've eaten in most of them!
L Do you speak Italian?
M Not much. I learned some at school, but I've forgotten most of it now, unfortunately. I'd like to learn again, because I really love Italian opera. I've been to the opera in Milan several times, and I've seen some of the best singers in the world. Do you like opera?
L No, I don't really like opera or any type of classical music. I prefer dance music and pop music. I really like a band called Arctic Fire.
M Oh, I've heard some of their albums. My brother likes them, too. And I agree with you – they're great. I like all kinds of music – rock music, jazz – anything! In fact, I think there are really only two types of music – good music and bad music!
L You're probably right.
M Have you *tried* listening to classical music? I think you usually need to hear pieces a few times before you can really understand them. When you know the music, you enjoy it more.
L That's interesting. I'm not sure it's true for pop music. I've bought albums because I liked one song, but when I've listened to them several times, I usually start to like other songs more.
M Well, maybe we can go to a classical concert together one day?
L Sure, if I can take you to see Arctic Fire, too.

Unit 12

▶ 12.01

1 In London, the accommodation is really expensive.
2 I've done a lot of sightseeing today.
3 I like living in the countryside.
4 We have a reservation for 7:30.

5 The nightlife in Barcelona was brilliant.
6 I love travelling to different countries.
7 That restaurant has fantastic food.
8 The scenery in Switzerland was amazing.

▶ 12.02

1 It was too cold to swim in the sea.
2 Would you like to have lunch in a café?
3 You should visit the Science Museum.
4 You should try the grilled fish – it's amazing!
5 You can walk to the theatre from the station.
6 The oldest building is the 14th-century castle.

▶ 12.03

RECEPTIONIST Hello. How can I help you?
GUEST I've got a reservation for three nights.
R Three nights? Your name, please?
G Henderson.
R Thank you. Yes, that's right ... Henderson. A single room for three nights.
G Great. Oh, what time is breakfast?
R It's from seven until ten in the dining room.
G And what time is check-out?
R It's at 12 o'clock on the day you leave.
G Oh, and one last thing. Is there a gym I can use?
R Yes, there is. It's on the top floor next to the spa.
G How much does it cost to use the gym?
R It's free of charge for our guests.
G OK, that's great.
R So here's your key. Enjoy your stay.
G Thanks.

▶ 12.04

1 **A** I've won a holiday in Thailand!
  B Have you? Wow! That's fantastic!
2 **A** Can I buy tickets here?
  B Yes, you can. They're €20 each.
3 **A** Is breakfast included?
  B Yes, it is. It's from 6:30 to 9:30 in the restaurant.
4 **A** I saw Jennifer Lawrence in a café yesterday!
  B Did you? Did you talk to her?
5 **A** Could I have four tickets, please?
  B Sure. That's £32, please.
6 **A** Can I pay by credit card?
  B Of course. Please insert your card here.
7 **A** She's going to get her husband a cat for his birthday.
  B Oh, really? I didn't know Aydan liked animals.
8 **A** How much is it for a ticket?
  B It's £10 for adults and £6 for children.

▶ 12.05

1 **A** I've won £1,000!
  B Oh, really?
2 **A** Thanks for all your help.
  B No problem.
3 **A** I'm hungry.
  B Me too. When's breakfast?

4 **A** I've missed the last train.
  B Have you?
5 **A** I went to Rome for the weekend.
  B Did you?
6 **A** Can you call me a taxi, please?
  B Certainly.
7 **A** There's a car park under the hotel.
  B How much is it?
8 **A** She's going to live in the USA.
  B Is she?
9 **A** I really like opera.
  B Do you?
10 **A** There's a really good café near my house.
   B What time does it open?

▶ 12.06

SOPHIE Hi, Emma.
EMMA Oh, hi Sophie. I'm glad I've seen you. I've got some amazing news! Annette is going to buy an island!
S No! How can you buy an island?
E Well, people sell them, just like anything else. It's a bit like buying a house.
S Oh, really? Where is it? And what's she going to do with it?
E It's somewhere in Canada, and I think she's going to build a holiday home there for her family.
S So she's not going to live there all the time?
E Oh, no! There's nothing there, really; just a small wood in the middle.
S It sounds a bit boring. She should buy one somewhere warmer. One with nice beaches.
E Well, for one thing, an island like that is probably much more expensive! But I don't think she's interested in that sort of thing anyway. She loves the countryside, and the scenery there is really beautiful. She showed me some photos. When you look across the water from the island, you can see mountains and waterfalls.
S How lovely! And how do you get to the island?
E Well, at the moment, there's a man who takes them over there in his boat, but they're going to buy their own boat. Then they can come and go when they want to.
S So, how much time are they going to spend there?
E As much as possible, I think, but first they have to build the house! That will take at least a year. And Annette's children have to be at school during term time.
S What are they going to do with the house when they're not there?
E I don't really know, but she said I can borrow it if I want to.
S Wow, that's fantastic! You should do that!
E Don't worry – I'm not going to miss a fantastic offer like that!

Acknowledgements

The authors and publishers acknowledge the following sources of copyright material and are grateful for the permissions granted. While every effort has been made, it has not always been possible to identify the sources of all the material used, or to trace all copyright holders. If any omissions are brought to our notice, we will be happy to include the appropriate acknowledgements on reprinting and in the next update to the digital edition, as applicable.

Key:
U = Unit.

Photographs:
All the following photographs are sourced from Getty Images.
U1: Marco Rubino/EyeEm; Jose Luis Pelaez Inc/The Image Bank/ Getty Images Plus; FG Trade/E+; NicolasMcComber/E+; Thomas Barwick/Stone; Nikada/E+; Hispanolistic/E+; Chaay_Tee/iStock/ Getty Images Plus; Orbon Alija/E+; Dean Mitchell/E+; Shapecharge/ E+; steve lundqvist photography/Moment Open; Morsa Images/ DigitalVision; JohnnyGreig/E+; Nirian/E+; **U2:** Courtney Hale/E+; Westend61; Gary Conner/Photodisc; Mel Yates/DigitalVision; Ron Levine/DigitalVision; R.M. Nunes/iStock/Getty Images Plus; PhotoAlto/ Eric Audras/PhotoAlto Agency RF Collections; ER Productions Limited/ DigitalVision; Hill Street Studios/DigitalVision; **U3:** Strauss/Curtis/The Image Bank; Yongyuan/E+; Jeffbergen/E+; David Pereiras/EyeEm; Neirfy/iStock/Getty Images Plus; William King/Taxi; Yuri_Arcurs/E+; **U4:** EmirMemedovski/E+; Blend Images - Peathegee Inc; **U5:** Yenwen/ E+; Ariel Skelley/DigitalVision; Dmytro Aksonov/E+; Tramino/iStock; _ultraforma_/E+; Georgeclerk/E+; Maremagnum/Corbis Documentary; Strickke/E+; Martin-dm/E+; Onurdongel/E+; **U6:** Steve Granitz/ WireImage; John Cumming/The Image Bank; Hybrid Images/ Cultura; Ariel Skelley/DigitalVision; Caiaimage; Maskot; **U7:** vinzo/ E+; DoraDalton/iStock Unreleased; Portra/E+; Vladimir Godnik; Oxygen/Moment; ajr_images/iStock/Getty Images Plus; Julian Elliott Photography/The Image Bank Unreleased; KJELL LINDER/Moment; vichie81/iStock/Getty Images Plus; Westend61; **U8:** Rachid Chbani/ EyeEm; Kolostock; Feedough/iStock/Getty Images Plus; RoBeDeRo/ E+; Bambu Productions/DigitalVision; Izusek/E+; Umkehrer/iStock/ Getty Images Plus; Razvan/iStock Editorial; GlobalStock/E+; Halfpoint/ iStock/Getty Images Plus; Mehmet Tay/EyeEm; **U9:** TommL/E+; Mint Images; Kopophoto/iStock Editorial; Csondy/E+; Vera Kevresan/ EyeEm; Portra/DigitalVision; filadendron/E+; Kali9/E+; Mixetto/iStock/ Getty Images Plus; andresr/E+; Tom Werner/DigitalVision; **U10:** Paul Bradbury/OJO Images; Photojournalis/iStock/Getty Images Plus; Martin Harvey; SDI Productions/E+; Plume Creative/DigitalVision; Ales-A/ E+; **U11:** Agencyby/iStock/Getty Images Plus; Witthaya Prasongsin/ Moment; Trio Images/DigitalVision; Lawrence Manning/Stone; Barros & Barros/Stone; Jianying yin/E+; Viktorcvetkovic/E+; Luoman/E+; SensorSpot/E+; Tara Moore/DigitalVision; Alberto E. Rodriguez/Getty Images Entertainment; Shapecharge/E+; **U12:** Manfred Gottschalk/The Image Bank Unreleased; Aimin Tang/Photographer's Choice; Image Source; AntonioGuillem/iStock/Getty Images Plus; LeonU/E+; Jelena Danilovic/iStock/Getty Images Plus.

The following photographs are sourced from another library.

U6: Julie Keen/Shutterstock; **U10**: Voronin76/Shutterstock; Samot/ Shutterstock.

Cover photography by Yaorusheng/Moment/Getty Images.

Commissioned photography by Gareth Boden: **U1**.

Illustrations:
QBS Learning; John Goodwin; Sean/KJA Artists; Alan/KJA Artists; John/KJA Artists; Dusan Lakicevic; Victoria Woodgate.

Commissioned Video stills by Rob Maidment and Sharp Focus Productions.

Filming in King's College by kind permission of the Provost and Scholars of King's College, Cambridge.

Audio production by Hart McLeod and by Creative Listening.

Typeset by QBS Learning.

Corpus
Development of this publication has made use of the Cambridge English Corpus (CEC). The CEC is a computer database of contemporary spoken and written English, which currently stands at over one billion words. It includes British English, American English and other varieties of English. It also includes the Cambridge Learner Corpus, developed in collaboration with the University of Cambridge ESOL Examinations. Cambridge University Press has built up the CEC to provide evidence about language use that helps us to produce better language teaching materials.

English Profile
This product is informed by English Vocabulary Profile, built as part of English Profile, a collaborative programme designed to enhance the learning, teaching and assessment of English worldwide. Its main funding partners are Cambridge University Press and Cambridge Assessment English and its aim is to create a 'profile' for English, linked to the Common European Framework of Reference for Languages (CEFR). English Profile outcomes, such as the English Vocabulary Profile, will provide detailed information about the language that learners can be expected to demonstrate at each CEFR level, offering a clear benchmark for learners' proficiency. For more information, please visit www.englishprofile.org.

CALD
The Cambridge Advanced Learner's Dictionary is the world's most widely used dictionary for learners of English. Including all the words and phrases that learners are likely to come across, it also has easy-to-understand definitions and example sentences to show how the word is used in context. The Cambridge Advanced Learner's Dictionary is available online at dictionary.cambridge.org.

CAMBRIDGE
UNIVERSITY PRESS

University Printing House, Cambridge CB2 8BS, United Kingdom

One Liberty Plaza, 20th Floor, New York, NY 10006, USA

477 Williamstown Road, Port Melbourne, VIC 3207, Australia

314–321, 3rd Floor, Plot 3, Splendor Forum, Jasola District Centre, New Delhi – 110025, India

103 Penang Road, #05-06/07, Visioncrest Commercial, Singapore 238467

Cambridge University Press is part of the University of Cambridge.

It furthers the University's mission by disseminating knowledge in the pursuit of education, learning and research at the highest international levels of excellence.

cambridge.org
Information on this title: cambridge.org/9781108962032

© Cambridge University Press 2022

First published 2022

20 19 18 17 16 15 14 13 12 11 10 9 8 7 6 5 4 3 2 1

Printed in Great Britain by Ashford Colour Press Ltd.

A catalogue record for this publication is available from the British Library

ISBN 978-1-108-96526-2 Elementary Student's Book with eBook
ISBN 978-1-108-96199-8 Elementary Student's Book with Digital Pack
ISBN 978-1-108-96202-5 Elementary Workbook with Answers
ISBN 978-1-108-96203-2 Elementary Workbook without Answers
ISBN 978-1-108-96200-1 Elementary Combo A with Digital Pack
ISBN 978-1-108-96201-8 Elementary Combo B with Digital Pack
ISBN 978-1-108-96204-9 Elementary Teacher's Book with Digital Pack
ISBN 978-1-108-96527-9 Elementary Presentation Plus
ISBN 978-1-009-11876-7 Elementary Student's Book with Digital Pack, Academic Skills and Reading Plus

Additional resources for this publication at cambridge.org/empower